CHILDREY

Introduction

When I first came back to the village of my childhood I was overjoyed to be coming home. I am the 4th generation of my family so I have many photos and letters inherited from my grandmother and my aunts. One day while I was sorting them into some sort of order an old school friend called in to see me and was really excited to see them and suggested that I publish them in a book and this is it. Many people brought me their treasured photos to be included, the eldest was nearly 90, and like everyone in this book, had attended one of the Childrey schools. I found it amazing that she identified nearly everybody on the photo which was a group of school children in 1923, what a fantastic memory! All but a few of the people in these photos went to Childrey schools Fettiplace and the Council School. This is not just a book of memories but a history of the last hundred years, for the children of the future to know where their past is firmly set. This book runs from the late 1800 to 1965-70 roughly, and God willing there will be a 2nd book as I was lucky enough to get dozens of photos more than would fit into the one book, one that was not too heavy to lift anyway.

I hope you enjoy it,

Jeanne Gibbs

Acknowledgements

First to all my school friends we had wonderful days of reminiscing when a five minute visit lasted hours. An immense thankyou to Mr I Rowland who has done all the inquiry work for me as I cannot get around, and he and his wife Barbara for transporting me to Reading to the Record Office and University who gave me permission to use the details and records I have used. To my friend and neighbour Mrs D Rowland for her encouragement and photos, also Mrs Sylvia Lay, Adrian Vaughan, Mrs June Young, Mrs Edna Harris, Mr and Mrs Bert Rowland, Mrs Mary Simmonds, Mrs Sylvia Rowland, Mrs Sylvia Jeffries, Mr D Legge, Mr M C Stevenson, Mr and Mrs J Devlin, Mr and Mrs R Floyd, Mr and Mrs Bert Rowland (Sen), Mrs S Whicker and family, The Rural History Centre, The University of Reading, Oxfordshire County Council Photography Archive, The Gazette and Herald and to anyone else I have inadvertantly forgotten.

If you have any information about the pictures in this book I would like to hear from you.

Author

Contents

Beginning at Holloway

Tanks coming down Holloway from Wantage in the 2nd World War years

You can just see the children on the right,
the smoke pots were placed to guide the tanks.

I wonder if the boy talking to the man on the bike is Bob Giles son of the landlord.

1961 approx. Mrs Gibbs with grandaughter Denise. John Collins with Steven? June Young sitting on her right. Mr Vaughan, lower right corner on road.

Morris Men and onlookers on the same day

Past the Crown the cottage next to it is now tiled, next is Wallington cottage which was pulled down 1938-9 and the present bungalow built

Mr & Mrs Wallington with daughter and grandson the man on the right unknown but is possibly Ealand Alder

Opposite on The green Mrs Broad, Elsie Rowlands grandmother with dog

Turning up West Street

Turning Left up West Street to School

The corner again with Mr Trinder's car coming down West Street. The men are Alan Bungay, Mr Simmonds

Childrey House West Street 1915
Corner Cottage in the background

This is where the cresent of council houses was built on the left approx 1947.
Somervilles Farm is the brick farm at the top left.
Isn't the cottage on the right unusual? it was pulled down in the early 1930's

A very important Lady

The last day of Mrs Mary Legges postal duties after 30 odd years, age 78 through all winds and weathers and two posts a day

Mrs Legge with her husband Harry Legge who was the village baker for many years, at the baptism of their grandchild

c 1915 Veor Farm West St. and Mrs Rea the Younger

Maltravers Manor West Street

Back veiw Maltravers Manor The misses Wickstead and Miss Tozer

Childrey School

This is the centre of the Village in my mind.
Nearly everyone passed through here.

Is your grand parent or parent in here?
Do you look like them? you might be surprised

The laurels are not very big here are they,
Mr Trinder dared us to get near them,
he was very fond of them.
They were much bigger in the 1930's

Miss Stevenson was a fovorite teacher this is her story sent to me by her nephews

Miss Hetty Frances Stevenson was born 1st July 1900 and died 7th April 1982 when she was 81. She was part of a long established Wantage family. Her father W C Stevenson was the Registrar of Births and Deaths at Wantage and Grandfather George Stevenson was an Ironmonger at Wantage and also the Engineer who set up the Wantage Tramway which opened in 1875.

She was educated at Alton House School, Wantage and left at the age of 14 with a glowing report from the Headteacher Miss C Bayley. She immediately became a "Pupil teacher" at the Wesleyan School in Church St., Wantage and after 4 years in 1918 enrolled at the Battersea Southlands Teacher Training College in London. Unfortunately she became ill with asthma (which she suffered all her life) and had to withdraw from the College. In those days you had to pay back the cost of the training and the college demanded £39 from her. As an alternative to paying this sum which was significant in those days the Board of Education wrote to her "The Board will allow you to discharge your obligation by service in approved schools for the period named in Clause of the Undertaking in lieu of repayment". The letter doesn't state what the period was but I doubt they intended it to be 41 years. I have her Appointment letter from Berkshire Education Committee showing that she commenced teaching at Childrey Mixed School 22nd September 1919 as an Assistant Teacher for a salary of £70 per annum. She retired from Childrey School after 41 years in July 1960. Mr Childerly was Headmaster when she left but Mr Trinder was there as Headmaster for 33 years in her time.

41 Years in the 'Happy Valley'

Farewell Gift to Childrey Teacher (see picture on page 27)

When presented with a radio on Thursday to mark her retirement after 41 years as teacher at Childrey School, Miss H. F. Stevenson, of 2 Charlton Park, Wantage, confessed that when she first started at the school she told her parents she would not stay there one month.

The presentation was made before a packed audience in the Reading Room, Childrey, by Mr. A. E. Trinder, of Swindon, who was headmaster at the school for 33 years until his retirement in December 1957, on behalf of past and present children, managers, staff, parents and friends. Mr K. F. Childerley, the present headmaster, introduced him.

Mr. Trinder recalled how Miss Stevenson had put the school before her own health. She always had the interest of the children and the school at heart and he had been grateful for the good teaching of Miss Stevenson, Miss Freeman and Mrs Hack, in dealing with girls when he was a "new boy" as the headmaster in 1924.

On behalf of the managers, the Rev. R. Collins (Rector) expressed their very best wishes to Miss Stevenson and regret that she was retiring.

After recalling her forecast that she would not stay a month, Miss Stevenson had stayed 41 years in the "happy valley," and she thanked the Childrey people for their co-operation.

Miss Stevenson was born in Wantage and started her career at the Old Wesleyan School in Church Street where she stayed for four years. She then had a year at home and then started her long association with Childrey School. She left on Tuesday before the end of term to start a holiday in Norway.

1920 Group 11

1 2 3 4 5 6
Back, Fred Isles ? Les Embling Doris Buckley Ernie Heading Margaret M. Dowse
7 8
Marjorie Booker Miss Stevenson
1 2 3 4 5 6 7 8
Front, ? ? Cyril Froud ? Donald Broad Janet Legge Tom Cox ?

1925 Teacher on right Miss Stevenson

1 2 3 4 5 6 7 8 9 10
Back, ? ? George Cox ? ? Ruth Legge ? Phillip Heading Tom Cox Les Embling
1 2 3 4 5 6 7 8 9 10 11 12 13
Middle, ? ? ? ? ? ? ? ? ? ? ? ? ?
1 2 3 4 5 6 7 8 9 10 11
Front, ? Ted Johnson ? ? ? ? ? ? ? ? ?

Photo taken after Oct 1921 Before summer 1922

1 2 3 4 5 6 7 8 9
Back, Daisy Welch ? ? ? ? Irene Marchant ? ? ?

1 2 3 4 5 6 7 8 9
Middle, Ivy O Bedford Kathleen Bedford Violet Legge Violet Booker Gwendoline Lewis ? ? ? ?

1 2 3 4 5 6
Front, ? ? Rose Winterbourne Olive Booker ? Poss. Marjorie Booker

1922-3

1 2 3 4 5 6 7 8
Back, Bob Heading Ernie Heading ? ? Les Embling Ernie Harris Frank Turner ?

1 2 3 4 5 6 7 8 9
Middle, George Barton Bill Barton Ted Barton Madge Buckley Violet Legge Rose Winterbourn Fred Isles Tom Cox Phillip Heading

1 2 3 4 5 6
Front, Len Barton Ruth Legge Pansy Legge Janet Legge ? ?

1 2 3 4 5 6
Sitting, Claude Burls ? ? Don Broad ? Don Green

Photo between Sept 1927 - July 1929

1 2 3 4 5 6 7
Back, Bert Harris ? Reg Bungay ? Gordon Booker ? Ben Legge

1 2 3 4 5 6 7 8 9 10 11
Middle, Peggy Freud Rose Freud ? Rose Clanfield Evelyn Greenhaugh Ruth Legge ? Phyllis Froud Madge Buckley ? Vi Turner

12 13
Nina or Nora Booker Jean Bungay

1 2 3 4 5 6 7 8
Front, ? Ted Johnson ? Edgar Barton ? Frank Johnson ? Dick Beckett

C 1930

Back 1 Marjorie Evans 2 Phillip Froud 3 Bob Evans 4 Phillis Barton 5 ? 6 ?

Middle 1 Pearl Hammond 2 Gordon Rowland 3 ? 4 ? 5 Mary Winterbourne 6 George Rowland 7 Sylvia Turner 8 Freda Bungay

Front 1 Ron Rowland 2 Phillis Breakspear 3 Derek Pointer 4 Nelly Booker? 5 Joyce Booker 6 Hilda Tomlin 7 Bert Rowland 8 ?

1936

Back, Doreen Alder [1] Phyllis Breakspear [2] Norah Clanfield [3] Stella Matthews [4] Mary Legge [5] Jean Evans [6] Mabel Sheather [7]

Middle, Alan Gibbs [1] Colin Matthews [2] Ken Gibbs [3] Bert Rowland [4] Ron Rowland [5] Ernest Evans [6] Bill Young [7] Ken Rowland [8] Fred Breakspeare [9] Joe Rowland [10] Jackie Rowland [11]

Front, Kathleen Matthews [1] Rose Clanfield [2] Joan Rowland [3] Phyllis Sheather [4] Iris Alder [5] Pat Alder [6] Peggy Rowland [7] Jean Evans [8] Barbara Gibbs [9] Mary Young [10]

Sitting, Brian Haines [1] Douglas Legge [2] John Sheather [3] Albert Rowland [4]

On the 1936 school photo

CYRIL JOHN (JACK) ROWLAND

Jack Rowland was the fourth son of Percy and Annie Rowland of West Street in Childrey. During the Second World War he enlisted as a private in the Suffolk Regiment. On D-Day, 6th June 1944, the Suffolks were part of the 8th Brigade in the 3rd Infantry Division which assaulted 'Sword Beach' in Normandy. The 8th Brigade landed near the town of La Breche and took part in the battle for Caen.

After the break-out from Caen, the Suffolks were engaged in the long fighting advance across northern France, which by the Autumn had reached The Netherlands. It was here that regrettably Jack was killed in action on 16th October 1944 aged only nineteen. He is buried in the Commonwealth War Cemetary at Venray.

C 1957

All these children are mentioned on other photos in the book

Vandervell Family
Dawn, Lorna, Danny, Stella.
C 1942

Teacher says Goodbye After 41Years Service

Mr Trinder handing over Miss Stevensons present

(see write up on page 18)

SPORTS DAYS 1960

From L-R Denise Rowland, Carol Young, Judith Rowland, Cheryl England.

Gill Wornham Winning the High Jump 1962

Prize giving 1962

Last day at Junior School 1963

Childrey Girls Football C 1963

1	2	3	4
Marleen Wheeler	Cheryl England	Carol Young	Linda Richens
5	6	7	
Judith Rowland	Janice Le Vinge	Denise Rowland	

School leaving photos No.1 1960

Back, 1 Steven Devlin, 2 James Aldridge, 3 Pauline Rowland, 4 Earnest Gaston, 5 Gerald Vaughan

Front, 1 Alison Chiderley, 2 Marilyn Gibbard, 3 Wendy Burls

School leaving photos No.2 1960-61

	1	2	3	4	5
Back,	Vic Cox	Les Rowland	Norman Smith	Michael Prior	Michael Stoneman
Front,	Christine Rowland	Susan Smith	Marion Young	Bobby Cheshire	Sandra Cully

School leaving photos No.3 1963

Back, 1 Gill Wornham, 2 Laurence Rowland, 3 Ryan Handcock, 4 Rita George, 5 Tony Floyd, 6 David Burls

Front, 1 Sally Legge, 2 Judith Bailey, 3 Rosemary Devlin, 4 Christine Read

School leaving photos No.4 1963-64

Back, 1 Peter Read, 2 John Joslin, 3 Alan Johnson, 4 Brian Smith

Front, 1 Carol Young, 2 Marlene Wheeler, 3 Linda Richens, 4 Cheryl England, 5 Janice Levinge

School leaving photos No.5 1966

Back, 1 Robin Simpson, 2 John Novis, 3 Dennis Gibbard, 4 Clifford Ledbury, 5 Paul Aldridge

Front, 1 Judith Rowland, 2 Carole Rowland, 3 Judy Joslin, 4 Fiona Simpson

School leaving photos No.6 1967

Back,	1	2	3	4	5
	Brian Levinge	?	Nigel Coules	?	Peter Johnson
Front,	1	2			
	Diane George	?			

School Registers
1913 - 1953

Contains all Fettiplace school children,
transferred to the council school,
the earliest born 1899

(1)

Admission No.	Date of Admission (or Re-Admission) Day	Mon.	Year	Full Name of Child	Name of Parent or Guardian	Address	What Exemption, if any, from Religious Instruction is Claimed?	Date of Birth Day	Mon.	Year	Name of Last School	Date of Last Attendance at this School Day	Mon.	Year	Cause of Leaving	Remarks
1	3	2	13	Wheeler Henry	Richard Wheeler	Childrey		18	3	99	Childrey Fettyplace	27	6	13	14 yrs of age.	
2	"	"	"	Wheeler Sidney	"	"		27	8	00	"	27	3	14	Left the Village.	
3	"	"	"	Pettifer Charles	Ernest Pettifer	"		4	9	99	"	8	8	13	14 yrs of Age	
4	"	"	"	Rowland Roberts	Charles Rowland	"		13	7	00	"	1	8	13	Age Exemption	
5	"	"	"	Rogers Herbert	John Rogers	W. Challow		31	7	00	"	4	4	13	Left the Village	
6	"	"	"	Marchant Wm.	Wm Marchant	Childrey		21	1	01	"	18	2	14	Form 5B. Attendc	
7	"	"	"	Barney Leonard	Broad	"		27	3	01	"	13	5	14	Form. 5B.	
8	"	"	"	Edmonds Albert	Mr Edmonds	"		28	4	01	"	13	5	14	Form 5 B	
9	"	"	"	Pointer Wm.	H Arthur Froude	"		8 / 3	10 / 4	02 / 01	"	2	10	14	Age (during week)	
10	"	"	"	Barrett Jesse	Arthur Barrett	"		3	9	01	"	19 / ~~4~~	3 / ~~12~~	15 / ~~14~~	Form 5B. / Left the Village	
11	"	"	"	Harman Alfred	Hy.	"		11	7	01	"	27	12	14	Left the Village	
12	"	"	"	Townsend Fred	Walter Jones	"		23	12	00	"	18	8	14	Form 5B. Attendc	
13	"	"	"	Fairchild Fred	Joseph Fairchild	"		26	2	00	"	20	6	13	Attendance Exemption	
14	"	"	"	Collins Albert	Thomas Collins	"		3	12	01	"	19	3	15	Form 5 B	
15	"	"	"	Burls John	John Burls	"		19	4	00	"	6	4	14	14 yrs of age	
16	"	"	*	Hatt Annie	Wm Hatt	"		26	10	99	"	7	3	13	For Work (Form Attendc)	
17	"	"	"	Hammond Nellie	Jas. Hammond	"		17	9	99	"	8	8	13	14 yrs of age.	
18	"	"	"	Townsend Elsie	Chas Townsend	W Challow		9	9	00	"	5	12	13	Age ~~Exemption~~	
19	"	"	"	Evans Winifred	Chas. Evans	W. Challow		9	10	99	"	10	10	13	14 yrs of age.	
20	"	"	"	Comley Ena	Fred Comley	Childrey		22	8	00	"	7	8	14	14 yrs of age	
21	"	"	"	Wearing Florence	Geo Comley	"		1	4	01	"	31	3	15	Age	
22	"	"	"	Young Mary	Geo. Young	"		30	8	01	"	6	8	15	Age (after holiday)	
23	"	"	"	Hermon Lena	Jas. Hermon	W. Challow		11	9	01	"	25	6	15	Form V b.	
24	"	"	"	Harman Elizabeth	Henry Harman	Childrey		14	4	03	"	4	12	14	Left the district	
25	"	"	"	Evans Louisa	Chas Evans	W. Challow		7	1	02	"	24	12	15	Age	
26	"	"	"	Townsend Daisy	Walter Jones	Childrey		22	7	02	"	5	11	15	Form V b.	
27	"	"	"	Booker Leslie	John Booker	"		5	4	02	"	30	4	15	Form V b.	
28	"	"	"	Harris William	Mr Harris	"		1	5	02	"	20	2	14	Left the Village	
29	"	"	"	Dance William	Eli Dance	"		23	11	02	"	14	4	16	Work Form V b.	
30	"	"	"	Rea Percy	Matthew Rea	"		2	7	03	"	30	6	16	Form 5B.	
31	"	"	"	Fairchild Walter	Joseph	"		21	5	02	"	21	5	15	Form 5B Attendance	
32	"	"	"	Pike Albert	Mr Rowland	"		9	12	01	"	17	3	14	Age on 9-12-15	Hospital since [illegible]
33	"	"	"	Griffiths Reg.	John Griffiths	"		12	6	03	"	8	[illegible]	[illegible]	Age	
34	"	"	"	Humphries Edgar	Thos. Humphries	"		6	8	03	"	8	8	13	Left the Village	
35	"	"	"	Fairchild George	Joseph	"		5	2	04	"	6	8	15	"	

(1)

Admission No.	Date of Admission (or Re-Admission) Day	Mon.	Year	Full Name of Child	Name of Parent or Guardian	Address	What Exemption, if any, from Religious Instruction is Claimed?	Date of Birth Day	Mon.	Year	Name of Last School	Date of Last Attendance at this School Day	Mon.	Year	Cause of Leaving	Remarks (2)
(2)																
36	3	2	13	Edmonds John	Mr Edmonds	Childrey		18	3	04	Childrey Fettyplace	28	3	17	Left 13 yrs old	
37	"	"	"	Young Frank	Geo. Young	"		31	5	04	" "					
38	"	"	"	Dance Arthur	Eli Dance	"		23	11	02	" "	14	4	16	Work Form V B.	
39	"	"	"	Pottinger Edgar	Geo. Pottinger	"		19	3	04	" "	30	3	17	Left 13 yrs	
40	"	"	"	Rogers Maurice	John Rogers	W. Challow		13	5	02	" "	4	4	13	Left the Village	
41	"	"	"	Winterbourne Fred	Geo. Winterbourne	Childrey		22	9	04	" "	12	10	17	13 yrs	
42	"	"	"	Newman Fred	Fred Newman	"		29	9	04	" "	9	10	17	13 yrs	
43	"	"	"	Stevens Fred	Henry Stevens	"		8	1	05	" "	11	8	16	Left ~~village~~.	
44	"	"	"	Treadwell Frank	Thos. Treadwell	"		21	4	05	" "	17	5	17	Left. 13 yrs.	
45	"	"	"	Rogers Tom	John Rogers	W. Challow		17	7	03	" "	4	4	13	Left the Village	
46	"	"	"	Humphries Cecil	Thos. Humphries	Childrey		1	8	05	" "	8	8	13	Left the Village	
47	"	"	"	Collins Percy	Thos Collins	"		13	8	05	" "	9	8	18	13 yrs.	
48	"	"	"	Dance Daisy	Geo. Dance	"		11	3	02	" "	10	3	16	Age.	
49	"	"	"	Burls Nellie (Louise)	John Burls	"		8	1	02	" "	8	1	16	Age	
50	"	"	"	Pointer Violet	Arthur Froude	"		7	12	02	" "	8	12	16	age.	
51	"	"	"	Hammond Emily	James Hammond	"		13	2	03	" "	19	1	17	Attendance	
52	"	"	"	Embling Mildred	Geo Embling	"		2	7	03	" "	29	6	17	" "	
53	"	"	"	Hopson Alice	Arthur Hopson	W. Challow		10	8	03	" "	19	12	13	Gone to East Challow	
54	"	"	"	Townsend Millie	Chas. Townsend	"		21	4	03	" "	9	6	13	Attendance (Form V B)	
55	"	"	"	Griffiths Winifred	John Griffiths	Childrey		15	6	04	" "	14	6	18	Age.	
56	"	"	"	Booker Lucy	John Booker	"		13	8	03	" "	13	11	16	Attendance	
57 Re	24	11	13	Marchant Kathleen	Wm Marchant	"		26	4	03	" "	25 15	4 8	17 13	14 yrs of age Left village for a time	
58 Re-a	27	10	13	Cox Ethel	Thos. Cox	"		12	9	03	" "	29 15	6 8	17 13	Left village Left the Village for a time	
59	"	"	"	Jones Winifred	Walter Jones	"		23	1	05	" "	24	1	19	14 yrs old	
60	"	"	"	Burls Irene	John Burls	"		8	3	05	" "	31	3	19	14 yrs old.	
61 re.	26	6	16	Hammond Elsie	Jas. Hammond	"		7	4	05	" "	17 7	4 6	19 16	14 yrs & attendance Left Village.	
62	"	"	"	Wearing Phyllis	Geo. Wearing	"		24	6	05	" "	8	8	19	Age	
63	"	"	"	Grafton Lilian	Chas. Stone	"		22	7	05	" "	~~22~~ 22 9	~~12~~ 12 1	~~17~~ 17 14	~~Attendance~~ Attendance Left the Village	
64	re-23	1	14	Douse Winifred	Fred Douse	"		19	9	04	" "					
65	"	"	"	Comley Florence	Fred Comley	"		5	9	05	Childrey Wes. Infts.	8	8	19	Age	
66	"	"	"	Booker Annie	John Booker	"		17	9	05	" "	8	8	19	Age	
67	"	"	"	Willoughby Gladys	Albert Willoughby	"		1	11	05	" "	21	1	14	Left the Village	
68	"	"	"	Iles Charles	Mr Iles	"		26	9	05	" "	4	10	18	(13 yrs)	
69	"	"	"	Cox Harold	Thos. Cox	"		14	12	05	" "	10	1	19	Age	
70	"	"	"	Townsend Anthony	Chas. Townsend	"		12	2	06	" "	19	10	17	Left village	

Admission No. (3)	Date of Admission (or Re-Admission) Day	Mon.	Year	Full Name of Child	Name of Parent or Guardian	Address	What Exemption, if any, from Religious Instruction is Claimed?	Date of Birth Day	Mon.	Year	Name of Last School	Date of Last Attendance at this School Day	Mon.	Year	Cause of Leaving	Remarks (3)
71	3	8	13	Rogers Harry	John Rogers	West Challow		27	2	06	Childrey Wes. Infs	4	4	13	Left the District	
72	"	"	"	Barrett Harry	Arthur Barrett	Childrey		22	5	06	" " "	5	9	17	Left village	
73	"	"	"	Winterbourne Albert	Geo. Winterbourne	Ch'd		15	6	06	" " "	4	7	19	Attendances	
74	"	"	"	Crane Florence	Geo. Crane	West Challow		11	4	05	" " "	2	5	19	Attendances	
75	"	"	"	Welch Annie	Wm Welch	Childrey		5	6	05		6	8	19	Age	
76	"	"	"	Marchant Maggie	Wm Marchant	"		30	11	05		19	12	19	Age	
77	"	"	"	Evans Lizzie	Chas. Evans	West Challow		23	12	05		19	12	19	"	
78	"	"	"	Lock May	Geo. Lock	Childrey		27	12	05		3	4	13	Left the Village	
79	"	"	"	Edmonds Winnie	Mrs Edmonds	"		18	1	06		31	8	20	Age.	
80	"	"	"	Newman Alfred	Fred Newman	"		13	5	06		3	1	17	Left village	
81	"	"	"	Douse Ernest	Fred Douse	"		21	5	06		6	6	19	Attendances	
82	"	"	"	Grafton Charles	c/o Mr Stone	~~W~~ "		4	6	07		29	7	21	Age	
83	"	"	"	Hopson Bessie	Arthur Hopson	W. Challow		23	1	06		19	12	13	Gone to E. Challow	
84	"	"	"	Froud Ivy	Edward Froud	Childrey		27	10	06		24	12	20	Age.	
85	"	"	"	Pettifer Vera	Ernest Pettifer	"		19	1	07		24	3	21	Age	
86	"	"	"	Jones Florence	Walter Jones	"		25	1	07		24	3	21	Age	
87	"	"	"	Embling Dorothy	Geo. Embling	"		22	4	07		29	7	21	Age	
88	"	"	"	Legge Joan	Ralph Legge	"		16	5	07		20	10	18	Attending Private Sch	
89	"	"	"	Heading Ethel	Robert Heading	"		18	5	07		8	8	19	St Catherines	
90	"	"	"	Young Margaret	Geo Young	"		2	6	07		29	7	21	Age	
91	"	"	"	Treadwell Irene	Thos. Treadwell	"		14	6	07		29	7	21	Age	
92	"	"	"	Burls Horace	John Burls	"		24	2	07		24	3	21	Age	
93	"	"	"	Booker Vaughan	John Booker	"		23	7	07		29	7	21	Age	
94	"	"	"	Cox William	Thos. Cox	"		4	3	07		24	3	21	Age	
95	15 "	10 "	17 "	Fairchild Dorothy	Joseph Fairchild	"		8	4	07		[illegible] 8	10 10	18 15	Left village Left the Village	
96	"	"	"	Hopson Gladys	Arthur Hopson	West Challow		7	5	07		19	12	13	Gone to E. Challow	
97	"	"	"	Douse Doris	Fred Douse	Childrey		26	7	07		29	7	21	Age	
98	"	"	"	Broad Ivy	Bert Broad	"		24	8	07		29	7	21	Age.	
99	"	"	"	Humphries Gladys	Thos. Humphries	"		30	8	07		8	8	13	Left the Village	
100	"	"	"	Pottinger May	Geo Pottinger	"		8	10	07		22	12	21	~~22~~ Age	
101	"	"	"	Marchant Irene	Wm. Marchant	"		27	12	07		22 14	2 10	21 21	Age Excused attendance	
102	[illegible]	1	14	Iles Doris	Mrs Iles	"		29	12	07		21	3	13	Left the Village	
103	"	"	"	Willis Willie	Wm Willis	"		14	2	08		25	7	13	Left the Village	
104	[illegible] 30 13	10.3 9 9	19 18 15	Bint Cyril	Thos Bint	"		4	2	08	19.1.19 24.3.[illegible]	9 17	8 2	18 15	" " " "	
105	"	"	"	Collins Ernest	Thos. Collins	"		12	2	08		31	3	22	Age.	

Admission No. (4)	Date of Admission (or Re-Admission) Day	Mon.	Year	Full Name of Child	Name of Parent or Guardian	Address	What Exemption, if any, from Religious Instruction, is Claimed?	Date of Birth Day	Mon.	Year	Name of Last School	Date of Last Attendance at this School Day	Mon.	Year	Cause of Leaving	Remarks (4)
106	10	2	13	Hutt. Wm. Geo. Hy.	Wm. Geo	Petwick Cottage	nil	15	11	'02	Goosey	31	3	14	Form V B. on 15-11-15	Excused 31-3-14 (Labour)
107	1	4	13	Burls Rosenia Ivy	John Burls	Childrey	"	17	5	08	none	4	8	22	Age	
108	1	4	13	Dance Albert John	Eli Dance	"	"	12	4	08	"	31	3	22	Age.	
109	1	4	13	Cox Maggie	Thos. Cox.	"	"	30	4	08	"	4	8	22	"	
110	1	4	13	Newman Florence	Frederick Newman	"	"	17	6	08	"	25	1	17	Left village	
111	21	4	13	Hunt Clarice, Emma	Frederick Hunt	"	"	15	1	'02	Sparsholt	6	6	13	Left the Village	
112	21	4	13	Hunt Frederick, John	" "	"	"	5	3	03		13	6	13	Left the Village	
113	21	4	13	Hunt Craven, Eustace	" "	"	"	7	2	05		13	6	13	Left the Village	
114	7	5	13	Pike John	c/o Mr Rowland	"	"	15	5	00	Credon Rd. Upton Pk.	15	5	14	Age	
115	14	5	13	Silk Ivy	Henry Silk	"	"	7	12	02	Wanborough	9	6	16	Form V B.	
116	14	5	13	Silk Doris			"	1	11	07	"	8	1	17	Left village	
117	15 / 14	9 / 5	14 / 13	Silk Elsie			"	20	6	05	"	27 / 17	1 / 7	17 / 14	Left Village for a time	
118	19	5	13	Townsend Ivy	Chas. Townsend	W. Challow	"	17	5	08	nil	12	10	17	Left village	
119	2	6	13	Johnson Constance Ethel	Reuben W Rowland	Childrey	"	20	4	05	Hinton Parva	13	6	13	Left the Village	
120	9	6	13	Turner ~~John~~ Chas	Albert Thos Allen	"	"	27	4	05	Wantage Nat. Boys	17	5	13	13 yrs.	
121	30	6	13	Evans James Claude	Frank	"	"	26	4	02	Kingston Lisle	21	4	16	Age during holiday	
122	15	9	13	Herman Oliver	James	W. Challow		8	10	08	Nil.	19	12	19	Gone to King Alfred's	
123	15	9	13	Froud Edward	Edward			21	12	08	"	21	12	22	Age.	
124	25 / 15	10 / 9	20 / 13	Welch Daisy	Wm.	Childrey		23	8	08	"	16 / 4	10 / 8	20 / 22	Left Village for a time / Age.	
125	15	9	13	Hammonds Gladys	James	"		10	10	08	"	21	12	22	Age	
126	15	9	13	Vasey Edith	Richard	W. Challow		12	3	03	Buscot	1	4	05	Left Village	
127	15	9	13	Simpson Olive May	L. Hammond.	Childrey		9	9	04	Bourton	24	10	13	Left the Village	
128	6	10	13	Stevens Herb. Ed.	c/o Mr Smith	"		26	4	02	Crondall Hants.	31	10	13	Left the district	
129	5	1	14	Griffiths Eliz. Mary	John Griffiths	Childrey		7	1	09	none	8	8	19	St. Catherine's	
130	5	1	14	Willoughby Leon. Albert	Albert Willoughby	"		6	3	09	none	21	1	14	Left the Village	
131	12	1	14	Norman Frederick	Wm. Norman			31 / 4	3 / 2	09	none	23	9	14	Left the Village	
132	24 / 19	9 / 1	17 / 14	Ballard Ed. James	Wm Ballard	W. Challow		4	2	09	"	12 / 31	2 / 3	20 / 15	Left the district / Gone to E. Challow	
133	26	1	14	Legge Ralph, Olaf	Ralph O. Legge	Childrey		29	1	09	"	20	12	18	Gone to G.S. Wantage	
134	30	3	14	Stroud James Alfred	James Stroud	West Challow		12	7	01	~~W~~ East Challow	9	10	14	Left the district	
135	"	"	"	Iles Gladys.	Mr Iles	~~Childrey~~ W Challow		5	2	09	none	19	2	23	Left the district	
136	1	4	14	Wearing Albert	Mr Wearing	Childrey		24	4	09	"	3	8	23	Age	
137	"	"	"	Broad Denis	F Broad	Childrey		25	4	09	"	3	8	23	Age	
138	"	"	"	Dance Charity	G. Dance	"		14	4	09	"	3	8	23	Age	
139	"	"	"	Booker Violet	J Booker	"		10	6	09	"	3	8	23	Age	
140	13 / 2	9 / 4	15 / 14	Skeats Ed. Wm	Ed. Skeats			29	6	09	"	4	5	15	Left Village for a time	

(5)

Admission No.	Date of Admission (or Re-Admission) Day	Mon.	Year	Full Name of Child	Name of Parent or Guardian	Address	What Exemption, if any, from Religious Instruction, is Claimed?	Date of Birth Day	Mon.	Year	Name of Last School	Date of Last Attendance at this School Day	Mon.	Year	Cause of Leaving	Remarks (5)
141	11	8	14	Wallis Abercrombie J.	Arthur J.	Kirklands' E. Challow	none.	30	12	05	S. Katharines Wantage	1	8	8	Free Place at G.S.	
142	3	6	14	Rowland Albert	D/o J. Rowland	"The Rest" Childrey		6	4	05	Upton	28	7	14	Left the Village	
143	3	6	14	Rowland Ernest	"	"		11	11	06	"	22/25	7	14	" " "	
144	22	6	14	Coxhead Sarah Ann	Wm. Geo Coxhead	West Challow	"	5	11	02	Coleshill	9	10	14	Left the district	
145	20	7	14	Woodley Wm	John Woodley	Childrey		8	12	00	Wantage Nat.	4	12	14	Age (during week)	
146	21	7	14	Coxhead Dorcas Rose	Wm Geo Coxhead	W. Challow		7	7	09	None	9	10	14	Left the district.	
147	18/27	10/7	15/14	Woodley George	John Woodley	Childrey		18	7	03	Wantage Natl.	6	8	15	Left district	
148	14	9	14	Douse Percival Wm	Fredk. Douse	"		19	12	09	None	20	12	23	Age.	[illegible]
149	"	"	"	Jeffery Wm	c/o Wm Marchant	"		27	12	07	Eastleigh	30	10	14	Left the district	
150	"	"	"	Kent Winifred Louisa	c/o Mr J Case	"		14	1	04	St Pauls Rotherhithe	4	12	14	" " "	
151	"	"	"	Jones Francis Edward	Walter Jones	"		4	12	09	none	20	12	23	Age.	
152	21	"	"	Silk Gladys Eliz	Henry Silk	"		4	11	09	"	[illegible]	[illegible]	16	Left village	
153	13	10	14	Gale Gladys Jane	Christopher Gale			30	12	03	Sparsholt	11	8	16	Left village	
154	13	10	14	Gale Winifred	Christopher Gale			16	11	05	"	11	8	16	"	
~~155~~	"	"	"	Davis Ernest	George Davis			24	1	07	Letcombe Bass					
155	13	10	14	Ogbourne Ernest Jas	c/o Geo Davis			24	1	07	Letcombe Bass	24/13	2/6	21/19	Age	wrong name brought by child verified later
156	14	10	14	Davis Ethel Florence	Geo. Wm. Davis			17	4	09	East Challow	11	8	16	Left village	
157	13/16	10/11	17/14	Fairchild Beatrice	Joseph			9	11	09	None	11/8	10/10	18/15	Left village / Left the Village	
158	"	"	"	Vass Hilda Annie	Octavius Jas. Vass			19	1	08	Waltham St Lawrence	14	1	17	14 yrs.	
159	"	"	"	Vass Ernest James	"			21	5	09	" "	1	8	19	Left the Village	
160	"	"	"	Shefford James Wm	Wm. Rob. Shefford			4	2	07	Ramsbury	24	3	21	Age.	
161	21/4	6/12	15/14	Collins Doris Gwen	c/o Mrs C Collins			20/15	7	07	Brightwalton	20/4	4/6	15/14	Left village / Left the Village	
162	5	1	15	Booker Olive May	Vaughan Booker			25	12	09	None	21	12	23	Age.	
163 Re	~~30~~ 18	~~5~~ 1	~~21~~ 15	Green Charles	Wm Green			31	3	04	E. Challow	~~31~~	~~-~~	~~21~~	~~Age~~ to Stanlake	
164 Re.	30	5	21	Green Joseph	"			13	1	08	"	17/12	2/2	22/15	Stanlake / Gone to live at E. Challow	Left 17/2/22 164 / Returned 6.1.19
165	"	"	"	Lewis Herbert Vaughan Samuel X	Sam. Geo.			20	12	05	Gt. Tiverton	10	1	19	13 yrs.	
166	25	1	15	Lewis Gwendoline Nellie X	"			18/23	9/12	09	"	21	12	23	Age.	
167	"	"	"	Lewis Lucy Dolly X				27	3	07	"	12	1	20	Gone to Private School	
168	8	2	15	Lewis John X				8	2	03	Bremhill	8	2	17	Work	
169	15	2	15	Lewis Annie X				14	11	04	"	31	5	18	13 yrs.	
170	1	3	15	Winterbourne Lilian Rose	George	~~George~~		21	3	10	None	21	12	23	Age.	
171 Re.	12	4	17/15	Winterbourne Walter	"			13	2	08	none	31/18	3/2	22/16	Age. / Left the Village	Readmitted [illegible]
172	19	4	15	Hunt Arthur David Sidney	Wm Hunt			13	10	09		21	9	23	Left the Village	
173	13	9	15	Cook Lydia May	Hy. Cook			17	11	02	Hatford	23	12	15	Gone to S. Kaths. Wantage	
174	"	"	"	Cox Thomas	Thos. Cox			8	9	10	none	24	7	24	Age.	

Admission No.	Date of Admission (or Re-Admission) Day	Mon.	Year	Full Name of Child	Name of Parent or Guardian	Address	What Exemption, if any, from Religious Instruction, is Claimed?	Date of Birth Day	Mon.	Year	Name of Last School	Date of Last Attendance at this School Day	Mon.	Year	Cause of Leaving	Remarks
175	13	9	15	Legge Violet Irene	Ernest Legge	Childrey	—	3	10	10	none	19	12	24	Age	
176	〃	〃	〃	Iles Fred	Mr Iles			3	10	10		19	12	24	Age	
177	〃	〃	〃	Newman Annie	Fred Newman			20	10	10		〃	1	17	Left village	
178	〃	〃	〃	Broad Olive Kate	Bert Broad			19	9	10		19	12	24	Age	
179 Re 19.3.18	〃 (8)	〃 (3)	〃 (18)	Bint Sylvia	Thos Bint			16	7	10		19.3.18 27 / 4	10 / 8	18 / 18	Left village / Left village	
180	〃	〃	〃	Johnson Arthur John	John Johnson	West Challow		8	9	10		29	7	24	Age	
181	27	9	15	Burls Edna Edith	John Burls	Childrey		13	12	10	none	19	12	19	Dead	
182	18	10	15	Hunter Charles	Joseph	〃		23	7	10	〃	10	10	19	Left Village	
183	26	10	15	Stroud Emily Olive	Geo Stroud	Lodge Farm Childrey		13	1	03	Linkenholt Hants	12	1	17	14 yrs of age	
184	10	1	16	Glover Olwen	Geo. Glover	West Challow		4	6	07	Private	1	8	18	Free Place at G.S.	
185	10	1	16	Gale Benj. Robert	Christ. Gale	Childrey		16	3	11	none	11	8	16	Left the village	
186	10	1	16	Heading Robt. Wm.	Robt Heading	〃		17	1	11		23	12	25	Age	
187	17 (9)	1 (5)	16 (16)	Collins Hubert	Jo Thos Collins	〃		8	7	10	Sparsholt	7 / 20	7 / 4	16 / 16	Left Village	
188	31	1	16	Embling Leslie Geo	Geo Embling	〃		28	1	11	none	10	4	25	Age	
189	21 (25)	2 (4)	16 (22)	Iles Mary	Wm Iles	West Challow		20	2	11	none	6 / 23	2 / 12	23 / 16	Gone to E Hanney / Left village	
190	3	4	16	Hunter Eliz. Annie	Wm Hunter	Childrey		1	6	11	none	31	3	22	Left Village	
191	〃	〃	〃	Davis Albert Ed.	Geo Davis	〃		16	6	11	〃	11	8	16	Left village	
192	〃	〃	〃	Booker Herbert	John Booker	〃		11	5	11	none	24	7	25	Age	
193	〃	〃	〃	Harris Ernest Geo.	Hy. Harris	〃		2	4	11	〃	5	6	25	Age	
194	〃	〃	〃	Froud Ellen Mary	Ed. Froud	〃		2	6	11	〃	14 / 11	1 / 8	21 / 18	Gone to S. Katharines Wantage / Left village	Returned 6.1.19
195	4 (19)	4 (6)	16 (18)	Pinnell Walter Leslie	Walter			22	6	11		9 / 1	8 / 4	18 / 17	attending private school / Left village	7.25 Age
196	15	5	16	Lambourne Lily	John			16	10	08	Sparsholt	9	8	18	Left village	
197 Re 8.4.18 Re 2.4.17	19 (28)	9 (9)	04 (16)	Nelson Edith	Agnes	Lodge Farm		19	9	04	Faringdon	20 / 27	10 / 10	18 / 16	14 yrs / Left village	
198	25	9	16	Legge Joseph Byron	Ralph	Post Office		20	8	11	None	24 / 18	7 / 10	25 / 16	Age / ~~Left~~ village	
199	26	9	16	Wright Harold	Elizabeth	Stowell C/O Mrs Woodl[illegible]		12	5	07	Faringdon	13	10	16	Left village	
200	25	9	16	Wright Edith Margaret	〃			11	6	10	〃	13	10	16	Left village	
201 Re	26 (12)	9 (11)	16 (17)	Bellinger Irene Ellen	Henry	Childrey		[illegible]	0	11	None	10	8	17	Left village	
202	25	9	16	Dowse Leslie Harry	Frederic	〃		7	12	11	〃	23	12	25	Age	
203	25	9	16	Turner Frank				17	9	11	〃	23	2	25	Age	
204	25	9	16	Lewis Irene	Samuel George	〃		19	11	11	〃	19	9	23	Gone to Private School	
205 Re	25 (23)	9 (9)	16 (18)	Winterbourne Walter	George	〃		13	2	08	Poppards	14	1	18	[illegible]	Re-admitted [illegible]
206	16	10	16	Stevens Fred	Henry	〃		8	1	05		22	3	18	13 yrs	Re-admitted 〃
207	16	10	16	Stevens Doris	Henry	〃		3	9	11		21	3	19	Left Village	〃
208	8	1	17	Richards Florence	Henry	〃		[illegible]	1	04	Letcombe	[illegible]	8	17	Left village	
209	8	1	17	Richards Gladys				7	2	06	〃	[illegible]	8	[illegible]		

Admission No.	Date of Admission (or Re-Admission) Day	Mon.	Year	Full Name of Child	Name of Parent or Guardian	Address	What Exemption, if any, from Religious Instruction, is Claimed?	Date of Birth Day	Mon.	Year	Name of Last School	Date of Last Attendance at this School Day	Mon.	Year	Cause of Leaving	Remarks
(7)																(7)
210	8	1	17	Richards Horace	Henry	Childrey			3	1908	[illegible]					
211	8	1	17	Richards Dolly	Henry	"			7	1911						
212	8	1	17	Heading Ernest	Robert	"		30	1	10		4	6	26	Age	
213	4	6	17	Rowland Mildred	Charles	"		25	6	11	[illegible]	28	7	26	Age	
214	5	6	17	Rowley [illegible]	[illegible]							24	10	24	To Aldbourne Wilts	
215	24	9	17	Buckler [illegible]	[illegible]	Challow		4	6	11	[illegible]	26	7	25	Age	
216	[illegible]			[illegible]				6	8	11		12	3	20	Left the District	
217	R 16 / 13 / 4	9 / 9 / 9	18 / 08 / 19	Molloy Charles Frederic	Patrick	Lime Tree Cottage Childrey		13	9	09	3 - 8 - 23 age	9 / 30 / 18	5 / 1 / 9	19 / 18 / 25	Left the Village / Left village / To King Alfreds School Wantage	29.7.21
218	11	3	18	Pennell Philip	Walter	The Bakery Childrey		5	2	13	None	9	8	18	Attending Private Sch	
219	11	3	18	Broad Donald	Hubert	The Green Childrey		16	1	13	"	14	4	27	Age	
220	11	3	18	Johnson Elizabeth	John	West Challow		5	2	13	"	14	4	27	Age. Taken off roll by medical & Attendance Authority received from Attendance Superintendent	
221	18	3	18	Barker ~~[illegible]~~ Marjorie	Vaughan	Childrey		1	11	12		4 / 16	2 / 7	26 / 24	To Wantage	
222	8	4	18	Bellinger Walter	Henry	Childrey		16	7	13	"	24	3	~~24~~	~~Left Village~~ Left Village	
223	8	4	18	Fawde Sybil	Richard	"		4	8	13	"	28	7	27	Age	
224	8	4	18	West George	Ada	"		11	6	13	"	7	10	19	Left Village	
225	8	4	18	Barron Margaret		"					"	4	5	18	Left village	
226	8	4	18	Jones Charles	Walter			18	6	13	"	6	11	25	To Wroughton nr Swindon	
227	17	6	18	Povey Doreen May	Mrs Dance	"		16	5	13	Grove	22	7	18	Left village	
228	29	7	18	Pinnell Kenneth	A. Pinnell	The Bakery Childrey		4	6	05	Edgewood Sd. Sonco	9	8	18	Left village	
229	23	9	18	Margaret Ivy Dowse	Frederic Dowse	Childrey		29	9	13	None	21	12	27	Age	
230	23	9	18	Legge Janet	Ralph	Post Office Childrey	R.	14 / 26	6 / 12	20 / 13	" x.	4 / 18 / 10	9 / 10 / 12	21 / 20 / 18	Left village / Left village } 30.5.28. Age. Left	
231	23	9	18	Stevens Agnes	Henry	Childrey		15	6	13		21	3	18	Left Village	
232	23 / 19	9	18	Rowland Herbert John	George	Stowell Childrey		19	11	13	"	21	1	27	To Lee-on-Solent temporarily	See Page 12 (Infants) Attending Lee-on-Solent Council School
233	30	9	18	Fake Daisy	Mrs Rowland	Cross Beds Childrey		10	12	13	Wantage	25	10	18	Left village	
234	14	10	18	Belcher Henry	Mildred Welch	West Challow		4	6	07	Wantage	20	1	19	Gone to Wantage	
235	14	10	18	Johnson Beatrice	May	Stowell		5	7	13	(West) Challow	25	10	18	Left village	
236	25	11	18	Doobridge Albert	Walter	High St. Childrey c/o Mrs King		27	4	10	Lower Caversham	30	11	18	Left village	
237	26	11	18	Ballard Frank	William	W. Challow		19	10	13	None	12	9	20	Left the District	
238	6 / 10	1 / 4	19 / 19	Higgs Thirza Annie	William	"		12	1	10	Wes. Wantage	6 / 6	4 / 4	23 / 26	Left for Worthing / Left Age	
239	6	1	19	" Rose		" "		26	9	12	" "	6	2	23	Left Village	
240	6	1	19	Buckley Doris	Eric	" "		25	10	13	None	5	4	24	Age	
241	R 6 / 22	1 / 9	19 / 22	Davis Phyllis	George	Childrey		4	2	14	"	14 / 21	10 / 4	21 / 22	Left Village / Left for Worthing	
242	13	1	19	Higgs Rachel	Wm.	W. Challow		29	9	08	Wes. Wantage	18	4	19	Left Village for a time	
243	27	1	19	Slatter Ernest	Ernest	Childrey		26		14	None	27	3	29	Age	
244	3	2	19	Head Wm.	Head Thos	Petwick		9	3	07	Uffington	4	4	19	Left District	

Admission No. 8	Date of Admission (or Re-Admission) Day	Mon.	Year	Full Name of Child	Name of Parent or Guardian	Address	What Exemption, if any, from Religious Instruction is Claimed?	Date of Birth Day	Mon.	Year	Name of Last School	Date of Last Attendance at this School Day	Mon.	Year	Cause of Leaving	Remarks (8)
245	3	2	19	Head Nancy	Thos.	Petwick		19	7	09	Uffington	4	4	19	Left district	
246	19	5	19	Dumbleton Frederic	James	"		10	5	06	Middleton	6 / 28	6 / 10	19 / 23	Attendances / left district	
247	19 / 9	5 / 3	19 / 21	Dumbleton Mercy	"	"		21	6	12	"	8	4	21	Left district for a time	
248	3	3	19	Cox George Cyril	Thos.	Childrey		19	2	14	None	29	3	28	Age	
249	1	4	19	Booker Ruby Priscilla	John	"		27	5	14	"	31	3	28	Age	
250	7	4	19	Hunt Frederick Ernest	Tom	"		17	4	14	"	21	9	23	Left the Village	
251	8	4	19	Burls Claude Vernon	John	"		7	5	14	"	2	8	28	Age	
252	12	5	19	Ryman Geoffrey	Raymond	Petwick Cottages		13	10	05	Didcot	8	8	19	Returned to Didcot	
253	20	5	19	Weston Phyllis Margaret	Fredk.	c/o Mrs Griffiths		10	3	10	Hinksey Oxon.	23	5	19	Returned Home	
254	2	6	19	Brown Margaret	Duke	c/o Mrs Stone		2	7	13	Chelsea	8	8	19	Returned Home	
255	26	6	19	Pinnell Kenneth Arch.	c/o Mr W Pinnell	Childrey		4	9	06	Ashbury	23	4	20	Left the District	
256	14	7	19	Belcher Walter John	c/o Mrs Tyles	"		28	8	11	Swindon	18	7	19	Returned Home	
257	14	7	19	Belcher Eileen Sylvia	"	"		29	6	14	"	18	7	19	" "	
258	16	7	19	Day Violet Christine	Arthur	Childrey		3	10	10	Wantage Natl.	3	3	20	Left the Country	
259	16	7	19	Day Winifred Ethel	"	"		30	4	14	"	3	3	20	" " "	
260	22	9	19	Mills Geoffrey Chas.	Ralph	"		27	6	14	None	21	12	22	" Cholsey	
261	22	9	19	Bartlett Amy	Ernest	Childrey		17	1	07	Buckland	14	3	21	Age	
262	22	9	19	Bartlett Edith	"	"		21	7	08	"	4 / 30	8 / 3	22 / 23	" / Gone to Goosey	
263	6 / 22	2 / 9	23 / 19	Franklin Dorothy	John	Petwick Cottages		15	5	14	Goosey	19	12	19	Gone to Goosey	
264	23	9	19	Pinnell Robert Geo.	Walter	"		17	11	14	none	2	11	27	To Cumberland [illegible] for holiday & attending there.	Re-admitted See Page. 13. [illegible]
265	24	9	19	Fullbrook Ethel Lena	Chas	c/o Mrs Rowland		3	1	09	W. Hendred	19	12	19	Gone to W. Hendred	
266	13	10	19	Belcher Ivy Gladys	George Belcher	Childrey		1	9	12	Uffington	31	3	20	Left Village	
267	13	10	19	Belcher Agnes May	"			21	6	10	"	31	3	20		
268	11	11	19	Evans Stanley Walter	Frank	W. Challow		19	3	14	Grove	21 / 31	11 / 12	19 / 24	Left Village / To [illegible] - [illegible]	To Lambourne.
269	3 / 6 / 14	4 / 1 / 9	24 / 20 / 23	Major Margaret Ellen	Charles	Childrey		26	3	14	Wokingham	23	6	22	Left Village	
270	6	1	20	Turner Violet	John	"		25	12	14	none	31	12	25	Age	
271	6	1	20	Hammond Greta	Richard	"		[illegible]	[illegible]	[illegible]		23	7	25	To Stanford in the Vale	
272	6	1	20	Legge Pansy	Ernest	"		10	12	14	none	21	12	28	Age	
273	13	4	20	Brewer Richard Vivian	Richard	Letcombe Bassett		7	1	08	Letcombe Bassett	13	4	22	14 yrs of age	
274	13	4	20	Greenough Evelyn Mary	Walter	Childrey		13	4	15	none	31	3	30	Age	
275	13	4	20	Rowland Sidney Ed.	Mrs C.	"		15	5	15	none	23	7	26	To Gosport	Re-admitted See Page. P12.
276	13	4	20	Barry James Walter	James	"		14	6	10	"	1	8	29	Age	
277	13	4	20	Barry Annie Mabel	"	"		14	6	15	"	"	"	"	"	
278	14	4	20	Clanfield Gwendoline	Geo.	West Challow		3	1	15	"	20	12	29	Age	
279	1 / 26	10 / 5	23 / 20	Brewer George	Richard	Letcombe Bassett		24	5	09	Letcombe Bass.	21 / 3	12 / 8	33 / 23	Age	

Admission No. 9	Date of Admission (or Re-Admission) Day	Mon.	Year	Full Name of Child	Name of Parent or Guardian	Address	What Exemption, if any, from Religious Instruction is Claimed?	Date of Birth Day	Mon.	Year	Name of Last School	Date of Last Attendance at this School Day	Mon.	Year	Cause of Leaving	Remarks
280	26	5	20	Belcher Sylvia	c/o Mr Tyler	Childrey	none	29	6	14	Swindon	28	5	20	Returned to Swindon	See Also Page 11
281	26	5	20	Belcher John	" "			28	8	"	"	28	5	20	" " "	
282	20	4	20	Wellington Sarah Drewitt	Robt.	"		20	7	08	Sparsholt	4	8	22	Age.	
283	"	"	"	Hunt Edith Ellen	Wm	"		19	11	15	None	21	9	23	Left Village	
284	"	"	"	Froud Phyllis	Arthur	"		5	10	15	"	19	7	29	Died.	
285	27	9	20	Wyatt Florence Lilian	c/o Mrs Green	West Challow		1	6	15	Marlborough	12	11	20	Returned home	
286	27	9	20	Johnson Francis Wm	Mr Johnson	" "		30	10	15	none.	17	4	30	Age.	
287	17	1	21	Booker Evelyn Norah	Vaughan Booker	Childrey		31	10	15	none	31	7	30	Age.	
288	"	"	"	Dowse Bertie	Fred Dowse	" "		13	1	16	"	30	1	28.	Removed to Wantage.	
289	5	4	21	Heading Philip	Robert Heading	"		29	2	16	"	2	8	28	To attend King Alfred School Wantage	
290	5	4	21	Legge Ruth, Margaret	Ralph Legge	"		18	7	16	"	30	1	31	Apprenticed as Pupil Teacher as from 1-2-31	
291	5	4	21	Froud Rose Alexandria	Edward Froud			21	6	16	"					
292	5	4	21	Davis Violet, Nellie	George Davis			21	7	16		31	3	31	Age.	
293	11	4	21	Hammonds Mabel Lena	Richard Hammonds	"		13	4	16	"	4	10	21	Left Village	
294	25	4	21	Major Percival, Albert	FredK. Major	"		17	3	16	"	23	7	26	To Stanford in Vale.	
295	27	6	21	Legge Margaret, Hilda	Henry Legge	"		6	10	15	[illegible]	23	6	22	Left Village	
296	5	9	21	Buckley Madeline	Mrs Buckley	West Challow		21	10	16	None	1	4	26	To Swanborough	
297	5	9	21	Cox George	George Cox	Childrey		26	4	16	Reading	24	1	32	Age.	
298	5	9	21	Hayes Rose	Wm. Hayes	West Challow		5	2	13	East Hendred	26	2	22	Returned to Reading	
299	6	9	21	Rogers Edward	Mrs Rogers	" "		1	10	10	Hampton London	30	9	21	Gone Home	
300	6	9	21	Rogers John	" "	" "		10	9	12	" "	25	10	21	Left district	
301	12	9	21	Arrowsmith Kitty	Wm Arrowsmith	" "		18	5	08	Lambourne	25	10	21	"	
302	12	9	21	" Florence	" "			31	1	10	"	29	9	22	Age.	
303	12	9	21	" Ida	" "			29	1	12	"	14	4	24.	Age.	
304	12	9	21	" Evelyn.	" "			27	4	14	"	27	3	29	Age.	
305	12	9	21	Rogers James				21	12	08	Hampton	25	10	21	Left district	
306	12	9	21	Green Donald	James Green	West Challow		5	4	15	Sparsholt	23	12	27	Left to proceed to King Alfreds School Wantage	
307	26	9	21	Bedford Ivy Olive	Wm Geo. Bedford	" "		30	10	07	Bletchley	22	12	21	Age.	
308	26	9	21	Bedford Kathleen, Grace	" "	" "		21	9	10	"	19	12	24	Age.	
309	16	11	21	Miriess Lily				26	7	14	Stanford	28	9	23	Left district	
310	9	1	22	Barton, William Richard	Mr J. [illegible]	[illegible]		[illegible]			[illegible]	31	5	23	Age.	
311	9	1	22	Barton Edward Chas				[illegible]			"	23	12	26	Age	
312	9	1	22	Barton Albert James				[illegible]			"	27	3	29	Age.	
313	9	1	22	Molloy, Milton, Henry	Mr M. Molloy			[illegible]			[illegible]	26	11	26	Removed to Whitbury Training Stables Mr Salisbury	
314	26	1	22	Arrowsmith Robert Thos.	Wm. Arrowsmith	W. Challow		5	10	16	none	[illegible]			[illegible]	

Admission No. 10	Date of Admission (or Re-Admission) Day	Mon.	Year	Full Name of Child	Name of Parent or Guardian	Address	What Exemption, if any, from Religious Instruction, is Claimed?	Date of Birth Day	Mon.	Year	Name of Last School	Date of Last Attendance at this School Day	Mon.	Year	Cause of Leaving	Remarks (10)
315	3	4	22	Johnson Edward	Mrs Johnson	W. Challow	[illegible]	9	4	1914	[illegible] none	30	7	31	Age	
316	25	4	22	Evans Stanley	c/o Mrs Evans	" "		19	3	1914	Grove	26	5	22	Returned to Grove	
317	25	4	22	Evans Lydia Frances	c/o Mrs Green	"		4	4	1917	none	26 / 13	5 / 10	22 / 23	Left District / Returned Home / readmitted	
318	25 / 25	4 / 4	22 / 23	Wallington Beatrice Rosalie	Mr Wallington	Childrey		14	3	1917	"	25 / 13	6 / 3	23 / 23	Left Village for a time	
319	25	4	22	Booker Gordon Fred[k]	John Booker	"		4	5	1917	"	29	[illegible]	31	Taken on as P.T. at this School [illegible]	
320	4	6	22	Turner Elsie	Mr Geo Turner	Swindon		1	12	1913	Jenning St Swindon	9	6	22	Returned Home	
321	12	6	22 / 25	Norman Daisy	c/o Mrs Welch	Childrey		28	8	1915	Sevenhampton	23 / 14	6 / 7	22 / 25	Returned Home / Returned Home	Re-admitted 9.6.25.
322	11	9	22	Barton Edgar Geo	John Barton	"		13	8	1914	None	12	10	31	Age.	
323	18	9	22	Lane Herbert Wm	c/o Y. Booker	"		14	9	1917	None	6	10	22	Returned Home	
324	9	1	23	Legge Raymond	Mr Breakspear	"		22	2	1918	"	1	4	26	To Sevenhampton	
325	10 / 5	4 / 10	23 / 25	Simms Joan, Ivy Doreen	Arthur Simms	Go Childrey		12	6	1918	"	22 / 15 / 21	11 / 3 / 3	25 / 25 / 24	To Kingston Lisle / To [illegible] Halford	
326	10	4	23	Legge Benjamin John	Ralph Legge	"		4	5	1918	"	29	7	32	Age	
327	10	4	23	Harris Albert Edward	Henry Harris	"		4	5	1918	"	29	7	32	"	
328	25	4	23	Wallington Olive Lilian	Mrs. Wallington			18	4	1918	"	25	6	23	Left the District	
329	30	4	23	Townsend, Edith May	c/o Mrs Jones	"		2	5	1918	"	6	4	26	To Wroughton nr Swindon.	
330	14	5	23	Bungay Reginald Eli	Wm Bungay	"		16	6	1916	Wanborough	31	7	30	Age.	
331	23	5	23	Bungay Florence Edith	" "			30	4	1918	none	29	7	32	Age.	
332	10	9	23	Richens Herb[t] John	Frank	W. Challow		28	10	18	"	22	12	32	Age.	
333	10	9	23	Rowland Edith May	Wm	Childrey		8	11	18	"	18	5	28	To West Ilsley School / Away for [illegible] with parent.	See Page 14
334	"	"	"	Shefford Arthur	Wm	"		5	11	18	"	6	12	27	Transf. to Reading with Mother. Attending "Battle" School	Readmitted See Page 13
335	"	"	"	Booker Nina Mary	Vaughan	"		25	7	18	"	23	12	32	Age	
336				Froud Margaret	Edward	"		22	9	18	"	23	12	32	Age.	
337				Maggs Gladys Bertha	Howard	W. Challow		25	5	18	Private	31	7	24	Reading Private School	
338				Butler Fred	c/o Mr Carpenter	" "		4	4	10	Croydon	19	10	23	Returned to Croydon	
339				Butler Charles	"	" "		11	11	11	"	19	10	23	" "	
340	14	9	23	Shillingford Priscilla	c/o Mr Breakspear			18	6	11		10	10	23	Returned Home	
341	12	11	23	Ward Derrick	c/o Mrs Marchant	Childrey		12	11	18	None	3	4	26		See Also Page 12.
342	8	1	24	Ballinger Francis Henry	Hy Ballinger	Orchard House Childrey		1	3	19	"	16	7	24	To Wantage.	
343		—	—	Green, Eric	Jas S. Green	Challow		25	11	18	"	3	8	34	Age.	
344		—	—	Green, Arthur James	Wm J. Green	" "		12	2	19	"	20	12	29	To Eaton Hastings	
345		—	—	Conley, Arthur Cyril	Geo Conley	High St Childrey		22	11	18	"	24	10	24	[illegible] Wilts	
346		—	—	[illegible] Ivy	Wm [illegible]	Challow		4	4	18	[illegible]	1	4	26	Left Age.	
347	14	1	24	Lewis Irene	Mrs E. Lewis	Childrey		19	11	11	Private	23	12	25	Age.	
348	5	3	24	Morton Albert	Mrs E Hunt	" "		25	1	14	[illegible] St London	[illegible]			Returned Home.	

Admission No. 11	Date of Admission (or Re-Admission) Day	Mon.	Year	Full Name of Child	Name of Parent or Guardian	Address	What Exemption, if any, from Religious Instruction, is Claimed?	Date of Birth Day	Mon.	Year	Name of Last School	Date of Last Attendance at this School Day	Mon.	Year	Cause of Leaving	Remarks (11)
349	1	4	24	Pottinger Wallace Eddie	Mrs G. Pottinger	West St.	None	9	5	1919	None	4	8	33	Age & Work	
280 ~~350~~	8 ~~29~~ 11	4 ~~4~~ 6	24	Belcher Sylvia	c/o Mr [illegible]	High St.	„	29	6	18	Ermin St. Swindon	20 / 17	6 / 4	24 / 24	~~Returned~~ to Swindon / Return to Swindon	See Also Page 9
350	29	4	24	Clanfield Wm Arthur	Mrs Clanfield	West [illegible]	„	10	5	19	None	15	9	33	Age & Work	
351	8	9	24	Barton Leonard	Mrs Barton	Council Houses [illegible]	„	17	12	19	None	24	11	33	Age.	Absent with S. Fever prior to leaving
352	14	10	24	Pittaway Kathleen	c/o Mrs Webb	Stowel	„	9	3	12	Kingston Lisle	19	12	24	To Fernham	
353	30 ~~9~~	10 ~~3~~	24 ~~11~~	Hotsfield Cecilia	c/o Mrs Harris	The Green	„	9	3	11	Stockbridge Council	11	11	24	To Stockbridge	
354	20	10	24	Broad Kathleen Fanny	c/o Mrs Broad	„	„	31	8	17	Battle Reading	20	1	25	Return To Reading	Re-admitted – see Page 12. (In Red)
355	20	10	24	Broad Norman	„	„	„	[illegible]	[illegible]	19	„	20	1	25	„	
356	15	12	24	Martin Eva Beatrice ~~Evelyn~~	c/o Mrs Bennett	„	„	28	2	14	Chepstowe	27	1	25	Returned Home.	
3587	6 ~~2~~	1 ~~10~~	25	Arrowsmith Jean	Mrs Arrowsmith	Council Houses W. Challow.	„	2	10	19	None	14	2	32	The Grove. Weddington [illegible]	
358	23	2	25	Birmingham Ruby	Mr Birmingham	West Str Childrey	„	1	10	13	Longcott	1	5	25	To Dorchester.	
359	23	2	25	Birmingham Violet	Do.	Do.	„	5	9	11	Longcot.	„	„	„	„	
360	2	3	25	Lee Lincoln H. V.	Mr Lee.	c/o Mrs Marchant	„	27	2	15	Gt. Coxwell	10	3	25	To Kingston Lisle	
361	2	3	25	Lee Gerald E. G.	„	„	„	17	7	18	„	10	3	25	„	
362	16	3	25	Mills Herbert	c/o Mrs Webb	Stowell	„	19	6	14	Rochester. St Margarets	17 ~~4~~	7	26	Returned Home.	
363	1	4	25	Barry Norah Mary	Mrs Barry	3 Council [illegible]	„				None	8	7	29	To Erith Kent & attending School there.	See Also Page 15
364	21	4	25	Molloy Eileen Mary	Mrs Molloy	Stowell	„	20	6	20	None	26	11	26	Removed to Whitsbury Stables Mr Salisbury.	Training
365	21	4	25	Booker Rosaline Nellie	Mrs Booker	West St.	„	26	2	20	None				Removed while in London.	See. Page 13.
366	21	4	25	Tomlin Gwen Lillian	Mrs Tomlin	High St.	„	11	7	20	None	14	3 ~~2~~	28	Away with [illegible] & when time to return to Stratton near Swindon owing to illness of mother	See Also Page. 14
367	21	4	25	Sly Mabel	Mrs Sly	Church St.	„				None	2	10	25	To Sutton Courtenay	
368	27	4	25	Froud Kenneth	Mrs Froud	The Hatchet	„	23	3	20	None	29	3	34	Age To Work	
369	6 / 28	10 / 4	25 / 25	Sims Gerald Arthur	Mrs Sims	Church Str.	„	25	5	20	None Swindon	23 / 18	11 / 9	25 / 25	Removed to Kingston Lisle / to Oxford ~~[illegible]~~ (Temp)	
370	1	6	25	Tilley Wm.	c/o Mr Wallington	High St. Childrey.	„	2	10	17	Gorse Hill	5	12	25	Return to Swindon.	Endeavour to introduce into Home. See lower in Red.
371	31	8	25	Page Nancy	Mrs Page	„ „	„	17	4	13		23	12	25	Winterbourne Rd Thornton Heath.	To Ashbury
372	„	„	„	Page Ada	„	„	„	24	5	15		23	12	25	Davidson Rd. East Croydon.	„
373	„	„	„	Page Charles Albert	„	„	„	15	8	16	Davidson Rd. East Croydon.	23	12	25	Ditto	„
374	„	„	„	Bungay Freda	Mrs Bungay	Chapel Cottages	„	5	12	20	None	[illegible]	[illegible]	34	[illegible]	
[illegible]	12	10	26	Simpson Henry	Mrs Simpson	Childrey	„	30	11	19	Uffington	8	10	25	To Fawler. ~~Uffing~~	
376	11	1	26	Pointer Ruby	Mr W. Pointer	„	„	11	1	21	None	18	4	35	Age	
377	11	1	26	Rowland Ronnie Mary Phyllis R.	Mr W. Rowland	„	„	28	12	20	„	18	5	28	To West Ilsley School for [illegible] – Holiday	See Also Page. 14
378	11	1	26	Turner Sylvia	Mr W. J. Turner	„	„	19	1	21	„	18	6	35	Age	
379	11	1	26	Legge Roger David	Mr R. O. Legge	„	„	29	3	21	„	20	12	35	Age.	A Girl not Boy.
370	16	2	26	Tilley Wm	c/o Mr Wallington	„	„	[illegible]	[illegible]	[illegible]	Childrey.	8	9	27	c/o Rev. Hodson Smith National Homes Highbury Park N. 5	Re admitted – No attendance made while away (Page 14)
380	22	2	26	Rogers Arthur	Henry John	„	„	21	7	13	Ashbury	24	3	27	To Uffington ?	
381	„	„	„	Rogers Violet Joan	„ „	„	„	9	6	19	„	24	3	27	„ „ ?	

Admission No. 12	Date of Admission (or Re-Admission) Day	Mon.	Year	Full Name of Child	Name of Parent or Guardian	Address	What Exemption, if any, from Religious Instruction is Claimed?	Date of Birth Day	Mon.	Year	Name of Last School	Date of Last Attendance at this School Day	Mon.	Year	Cause of Leaving	Remarks (12)
381	13	4	26	Winterbourne Rita Mary	Mr G. Winterbourne	West St. Childrey	None	15	4	21	—	14	7	35	Age.	
382	1	4	26	Evans Robert Reginald	Mr R. Evans	West Challow	—	26	5	21	—	1	8	35	Age.	
383	1	4	26	Green May	Mr W. Green	" "	—	7	5	21	—	20	12	24	Removed to Eaton Hastings, Faringdon.	
385	7	6	26	Partridge Winifred	Mrs Partridge	c/o Mrs Stone Stowell	—	26	12	20	Wilson School Reading	11	6	26	Returned to Reading	
354	14	6	26	Broad Kathleen	c/o Mrs Fleetwood	Stowell Childrey	—	31	8	17	Girls National Slough	23	7	26	Returned to Slough	See Also Page. 71
386	21	6	26	Daly Gerald Nolan Sinclair	Mrs Daly	West St.	—	21	8	20	—	13	10	26	Removed to Gloucester	
387	"	"	"	Anderton Edna May	Mr Anderton	Packer's Orchard	—	1	5	20	?	17	12	26	Removed to Hawkesbury?	Caravan People
388	"	"	"	Anderton Kathleen	"		—	22	5	18	?	4	12	26		
389	12	7	26	Lovey Dorothy	c/o Mrs G. Dance	Hatchet Lane Childrey	—	11	9	16	Grove	16	7	26	Returned to Grove.	
390	30	8	26	Pinnell Thomas	Mr W. Pinnell	High St. "	—	25	8	21	—	11	5	28	[illegible] Orthopaedic Hospital Reading [illegible] & Removed from Roll.	See Also Page 14. (Authority [illegible] 11/5/28)
391	"	"	"	Dowse Leonard	Mr F. Dowse	" "	—	21	7	21	—	31	1	28	Removed to Wantage.	
392	"	"	"	Jacklin Dennis	c/o Mrs G. Rowland	" "	—	2	9	21	—	4	10	29	To Faringdon Council School.	See Page. 15
393	"	"	"	Hammond Pearl Ellen	Mr J. Hammond	" "	—	24	5	21	—	11	7	35	Age.	
394	"	"	"	Booker Joyce Hilda	Mr V. Booker	Chapel Cottages "	—	11	7	21	—	1	8	35	Age.	
395	6	9	26	Wyatt Florence L. (Frances L.)	c/o Mrs Clanfield West Challow.	West Challow.	—	4	4	14	Lockridge nr Marlborough Wilts	1	10	26	Returned to Lockridge (Stockbridge)	See Below. (In Red). Re-admission
396	"	"	"	Wyatt Edmund			—	14	10	19		12	9	26	"	See Below. } See Also Page 13
397	"	"	"	Wyatt Wm. J.	"		—	"	"	21	"	"	"	"	"	See Below.
398	20	9	26	Edmonds Frank K.	c/o Mrs Kench	Stowell Childrey		18	2	20	Coventry Rd. Bulwell Notts	14	10	26	Returned to Bulwell (Coventry)	See Below.
399	21	9	26	Richards Clifford	Mrs Richards c/o Mrs Broad	The Green "		1	10	16	Boys Council Ton Pentre (Wales)	5	11	26	Removed to Stanford in Vale	
400	27	9	26	Richards Norman	"	" "		12	12	12	Pentre Secondary School	5	11	26	Ditto.	
401	6	10	26	Comley Gwendoline	Mr Sparrowhawk (Comley)	Godfrey's Farm Childrey	—	28	3	14	Buscot Berks	7	10	26	Removed to Woodhill Farm East Challow.	
402	18	10	26	Sparrowhawk Vincent G.	"	" "		24	5	21	" "	"	"	"		
395	23	11	26	Wyatt Florence L.	c/o Mrs Clanfield. W. Challow	West Challow.	—	4	4	14	Lockridge Marlborough	23	12	26	Returned to Lockridge!	Wantage? See Above.
396	30	11	26	Wyatt Edmund	"	"	—	14	10	19	" "	"	"	"	" " " ?	See Above } See R.
397	"	"	"	Wyatt Wm. J.	"	"	—	4	1	21	" "	"	"	"	" " " ?	See Above }
398	13	12	26	Edmonds Frank	c/o Mrs Kench	Stowell	—	12	2	20	Coventry Rd. Bulwell Notts	"	"	"	Returned to Bulwell.	See Above.
403 (99)	11	1	27	Green Denis Spencer	Mr J. Green	" " "		7	11	21	Nil.	8	6	36	Age. To Employment Challow.	
341	"	"	"	Ward Derrick	c/o Mrs Marchant	West St. "		12	11	18		16	3	27	To Boys' Home Farningham? Swanley Kent.	See Also Page 10.
404	31	1	27	Tilley Marjorie	Mrs Tilley	c/o Mr Wallington "	—	28	1	21		8	9	27	c/o Mrs Winfield Foxcote Kingham. Oxon	See also Page 16 & 18. Boy here, not girl. Alverstoke Children's Home School Gosport.
232	21	2	27	Rowland Herbert	Mrs Haines	Stowell "	—	19	11	13	Council School Lee-on-Solent	23	12	27	Age.	See Also Page 7
275	"	"	"	Rowland Sidney		" "	—	15	5	15	"	1	8	29	Age.	See also Page. 8
405	28	3	27	Rowland Thomas Gordon	Mr E. Rowland	" "	—	17	8	21	Sparsholt C. of E.	28	7	27	School Holidays then to Workington Cumberland on Holiday	Re-admitted see P. 13 (In Red).
406	1	4	27	Barton Phyllis Lillian Gladys	Mr Barton	1 Council Houses Childrey	—	11	7	22	Nil.	15	6	36	To Larkfield Estate. Larkfield Kent.	attending Senior Mixed Dept Central School – Snodland Kent
407	1	4	27	Breakspear Phyllis May	Mr F. Breakspear	Stowell	—	30	2	22	Nil	30	7	36	Age	
408	1	4	27	Legge Ivy Margaret	Mr E. Legge	"	—	[illegible]	[illegible]	[illegible]	Nil	"	"	"	Age.	

Admission No. 13	Date of Admission (or Re-Admission). Day	Mon.	Year	Full Name of Child.		Name of Parent or Guardian.	Address.	What Exemption, if any, from Religious Instruction is Claimed?	Date of Birth. Day	Mon.	Year	Name of Last School.	Date of Last Attendance at this School. Day	Mon.	Year	Cause of Leaving.	Remarks.
409	4	4	27	Ponting (Bunting struck out)	Hilda	Mr J. Ponting	Dog Lane Childrey	None	13	7	16	Lechlade Glos	10	10	28	To Sparsholt	
410	"	"	"	Ponting	Charles	"	" " "	–	31	10	20	" "	10	10	21	To Sparsholt	
411	26	4	27	Churcher	Doris E.	Mr Read	West St.	–	17	11	17	Council School Epsom	10	6	27	Returned to Epsom	
412	"	"	"	Holman	Helen S.	Mr F. Holman	West Challow	–	23	12	13	East Challow C of E	30	3	28	Age.	
413	"	"	"	Holman	Patricia A.	"	"	–	17	3	15	" " "	4	5	27	Age.	
414	"	"	"	Holman	Ralph E.	"	"	–	11	8	26	" " "	7	0	29	[struck out] ? Direct Council School. Removed from District (Home – Appleford.)	
415	"	"	"	Holman	Frank & Gordon	"	"	–	23	4	20	" " "	"	"	"	Appleford C of E.	
416	16	5	27	Sargeant	Richard	c/o Mrs Marchant	West St. Childrey	–	30	6	18	St. Peter's School Vauxhall	21	7	27	Returned Vauxhall.	
417	19	5	27	Evans	James	c/o Mrs Gran	West Challow	–	26	11	20	Norton School Birmingham	11	6	27	Returned to Birmingham	
418	"	"	"	Evans	Marjorie	"	" "	–	6	5	22		"	"	"	Ditto	
395	11	7	27	Wyatt	Florence	c/o Mrs Clanfield	West Challow	–	4	4	14	Fyfield Berks (Marlborough Wilts)	28	7	27	Moved to other Relatives – Staying at Wantage.	See also Pages. 12.
396	"	"	"	Wyatt	Edmund	"	" "	–	14	10	19	" "	"	"	"		
397	"	"	"	Wyatt	Wm J.	"	" "	–	4	1	21	" "	"	"	"		
419	5	9	27	Beckett	Charlie Thomas	Thomas Beckett	West Challow	–	7	8	14	East Challow	10	9	28	Age.	
420	[struck out]	9	"	Beckett	John Lawrence	" "	" "	–	22	9	17	" "	22	6	32	Age. [illegible]	
421	"	"	"	Beckett	Edith Jane	" "	" "	–	23	1	20	" "	23	12	33	Age.	Absent with S. Fever prior to leaving
422	"	"	"	Rees	Kathleen	c/o Mrs Marchant		–	15	7	18	Southampton St. Camberwell	14	10	27	Returned Home	
423	"	"	"	Allison	Patrick	c/o Mr E. Froud	Kilaire	–	17	3	20	Private School Colwyn Bay Denbigh	13	9	27	Returned Home.	
424	"	"	" x	Matthews	Mary	Mr G. Matthews	Lodge Farm	–	17	9	21	Baulking	8	8	33	Scholarship to Faringdon County Girls	
425	"	"	"	Cox	Marian	Mr T. Cox	Council Houses Childrey	–	20	9	22	Nil.	21	4	28	to East Challow.	
426	"	"	"	Pointer	Derrick Wm.	Mr W. Pointer	High St. "	–	25	10	22	"	21	5	37	Age.	
427	"	"	"	Froud	Philip	Mr E. Froud	Pond House	–	14	11	22	"	16	4	33	To King Alfred's School Wantage.	
428	"	"	"	Rowland	George E.	Mr S. Rowland	Stowell	–	27	10	22	"	6 / 27	5 / 9	32 / 37	Dec. Deceased.	
429	"	"	"	Barry	Kathleen Margaret	Mr J. Barry	Council House W. Challow	–	26	6	22	"	30	7	36	Age.	
430	"	"	"	Arrowsmith	Iris	Mr W. Arrowsmith		–	20	7	22	"	14	2	33	To The Grove, Headington Oxon. With	
431	"	"	"	Tomlin	Hilda Joyce	Mr H. Tomlin	High St. Childrey	–	15 / 24	9 / 5	22 / 28	To Baulking Pro Tem. & attending School there.	24	5	28	To Baulking Pro Tem attending School there	See also Page 15.
432	"	"	"	Rowland	Ronald George	Mr P. Rowland	West " "	–	24	8	22	Nil.	20	7	36	Age	
433	"	"	"	Rowland	Albert Wm.	" "	" "	–	"	"	"		"	"	"	Age.	
365	"	"	"	Booker	Rosalie	Mr J. Booker	" " "	–	26	1	20	Childrey	24	3	34	Age.	Away out of Area Sick See Page. 11.
406	27	9	27	Rowland	Gordon	Mr E. Rowland		–	1	1	3		1	1	3	Age.	See Page. 12.
434	24	10	27	Young	Eileen	c/o Mrs Young	"	–				Hanney	4	11	27	Returned Home to Hanney	
435	"	"	"	Young	Donald	c/o Mrs Young	Stowell	–		1	22	"	4	11	27	Returned Home to Hanney	
436	21	11	27	Pearce	Edith May	Mrs E. Pearce	"	–	1	12	28	Uffington	28	1	30	To Uffington	
264	10	1	28	Pinnell	Robert	Walter Pinnell	High St.	[illegible]	17	[illegible]	[illegible]	Sandhurst Council (Boarding holiday)	21	12	35	Age	See also Page [illegible]
334	10	1	28	Shefford	Arthur	William	Stowell "	[illegible]	[illegible]	[illegible]	[illegible]	[illegible] Reading	[illegible]	[illegible]	30	Removed to Shefford in Vale	See [illegible]

Admission No.	Date of Admission (or Re-Admission).			Full Name of Child.	Name of Parent or Guardian.	Address.	What Exemption, if any, from Religious Instruction, is Claimed?	Date of Birth.			Name of Last School.	Date of Last Attendance at this School.			Cause of Leaving.	Remarks.
14	Day.	Mon.	Year.					Day.	Mon.	Year.		Day.	Mon.	Year.		14
370	16	1	28	Tilley Wm.	c/o Mr Wallington	High St. Childrey	—	2	11	17	Idbury.	1	8	29.	Left District. Gone to — Aston Tirrold School	See Also Page 11. (Two Entries) " " 15
437	15	2	28	Martin John	c/o Mrs Marchant	West St. Childrey	R.C.	1	12	16.	St. Georges R.C. London S.E.1.	4	4	28	Returned Home.	
438	1	4	28	Clanfield Norah Amy	Mr A. Clanfield	West Challow	—	2	3	23	Nil.	25	3	37	Age.	
439	17	4	28	Hewlett Mona Irene	Mr E. Hewlett	High St. Childrey	None.	25	6	23	Nil.	28	7	38	Age.	
366.	21	5	28	Tomlin Gwendoline	Mr H. Tomlin	High St. Childrey	None.	11	7	20	Returned from Stratton St Margaret.	2	8	34	Age.	See Also Page. 11
333	30	5	28	Rowland Edith May	Mr Wm. Rowland	Council Houses " "	None.	8	11	18	Returned from West Ilsley	23	12	32	Age.	See Page. 10.
377	"	"	"	Rowland Phyllis	" " "	" " "	"	28	12	20	"	22	11	34	Age. (Excluded for [illegible] from 22.?.34 – [illegible]) Free Place.	See Page. 11
440	11	6	28	Adams Hugh Edward	Mr Adams	Blowing Stone Cottages	"	15	10	19	Greenwich Royal Hill Bl. School (S.E.)	17	10	30.	To King Alfred's School Wantage	
441	"	"	"	Adams Ruth	" "	" " "	"	15	1	21	Greenwich Royal Hill C.P. School	19	12	30	To [illegible] Norfolk.	
442	21	6	28.	Bevan Stella	Mr A. Bevan	High St. Childrey	—	23	6	15	Braywick nr Maidenhead Berks	3	6	29.	To Burford St Michaels Oxon.	
443	"	"	"	Bevan James	" " "	" " "	"	10	8	19	Holyport C of E.	4	6	29	"	
444	"	"	"	Bevan George	" " "	" " "	"	21	11	21	Holyport C of E.	4	6	29	"	
431	25	6	28	Tomlin Hilda	Mr H. Tomlin	" " "	"	15	9	22.	Baulking. C.	30	7	29.	To Newton nr Idbury to relatives (Two Entries).	See Page. 13 & 15
445	10	9	28	Mahoney John Anthony	Mr J. Mahoney	" " "	R.C.	20	8	20	Letcombe Regis	21	12	28.	To Salesian College. Battersea. S.W. 11.	
446	"	"	"	Mahoney Mary	" " "	" " "	"	22	3	22	" "	17	5	29	Convent School Chertsey.	
447	"	"	"	Mahoney Kathleen Cecilia	" " "	" " "	"	7	8	23	Nil. "	"	"	"	} "	
448	"	"	"	Young William George	Mr C. Young	West Challow	None.	17	10	23	"	22	12	37	Reached 14 yrs of age.	
449	"	"	"	Evans Mary Jean	Mr R. Evans	" "	"	22	9	23	"	22	12	37.	Reached 14 yrs of age.	
450	"	"	"	Pointer Marion	Mr W. Pointer	High St. Childrey	"	3	11	23	"	18	6	37	To Didcot.	
451	"	"	"	Panting Jack.	Mr W. Panting	Stowell "	"	4	10	23	"	24	11	33	Deceased. – [illegible] 1.?.34	[illegible]
452	"	"	"	Jacklin Eileen Joyce	c/o Mr G. Rowland	High St. "	"	7	11	23	"	4	10	29.	To Faringdon Council School.	See Also Page 15
453	"	"	"	Sheather Mabel Elizabeth	Mr J. Sheather	Stowell "	"	1	12	23	"	22	12	37	Reached 14 years of age.	
454	"	"	"	Walker James Henry	Mr R. Walker	Chave's [illegible]	"	8	5	23	"	30	7	31	Attending School at Radnage. Bucks.	
455	"	"	"	Alder Doreen Lillian	Mr J. Alder	High St. Childrey	"	10	11	23	"	22	12.	37.	Reached 14 years of age.	
456	"	"	"	Barry Agnes	Mr J. Barry	West Challow "	"	30	11	23	"	22	12	37	Reached 14 years of age.	
390	"	"	"	Pinnell Thomas	Mr W. Pinnell	High St. Childrey	"	25	8	21.	Orthopaedic Hospital Headington	21	12	28	Miss Bailey. To Private School Wantage	See Page 12.
457	24	9	28.	Lane Lewis Frank.	c/o Mrs Lewis	Chapel Cottages "	Nil.	21	9	19.	Palmer School Wokingham	5	10	28	Returned Home.	
458.	1	10	28.	Burton Margaret Elizabeth	Mr G. Burton	West St. "	"	12	2	17	Girls Council Newbury.	22	6	31	Age.	
459	"	"	"	Burton Evelyn Annie	" "	" " "	"	21	3	20	" " "	25	6	31.	Staying at Kenilworth nr Leamington Warwick pro tem & attending School there.	
460	15	10	28	Newton Sydney	Mr A. Newton	Dog Lane "	"	8	9	14	Farnborough C of E.	23	7	30	Age.	
461	8 / 8	1 / 2	29 / 29	Pearce Freda Pearl	Mr E. Pearce	Stowell "	"	[illegible]	2	[illegible]	Nil.	28	1	30	To Uffington	
462	8	1	29	Booker Margaret Joan	Mr J. Booker	West St. "	"	12	1	20	"	14	4	35.	Age.	
463	"	"	"	Rowland Kenneth Percy	Mr P. Rowland	" " "	"	20	2	24.	"	3	8	39	Age.	
464	"			Rowland Dorothy Myra	Mr S. Rowland	" " "	"	11	2	22	"	1	8	29.	To London Pro Tem. & attending School	Bromley Hall Rd School Allen Rd Poplar E.14 (See Page 15)
465	14	1	29	Lane Albert Edward	c/o Mr C. Pettifer	Stowell "	"	20	9	13	Letcombe	27	3	29	Returned to Letcombe Bassett	

Admission No. 15	Date of Admission (or Re-Admission) Day	Mon.	Year	Full Name of Child	Name of Parent or Guardian	Address	Exemption, if any, from Religious Instruction, Claimed?	Date of Birth Day	Mon.	Year	Name of Last School	Date of Last Attendance at this School Day	Mon.	Year	Cause of Leaving	Remarks 15
							None	5	1	24	NIL	30	7	36	To Faringdon County Girls.	
466	9	4	29	Matthews Stella Mary	Mr G. Matthews	Lodge Farm Chiswell	—	5	1	24	—	30	7	36	To Faringdon County Girls School	
467	16	4	29	Collingbourne Kathleen Mary	Mr R. Collingbourne	East Challow		27	7	23	—	31	1	30	Removed to Grove.	
468	9	9	29	Massey M.	Mrs Bedford	West [illegible]		1	9	24	—	29	9	29	Removed to Ashdown. To Lambourne School	only 3 weeks.
469	"	"	"	Bleier Hilda	c/o Mrs Green	West Challow.	—	2	3	21	Wood Close London.	8	9	29	Returned Home.	
470	"	"	"	Sherbourne Doreen	c/o Mrs Wain	Childrey		27	2	21	Radfield Bristol.	8	9	29	Returned home	
471	"	"	"	Sherbourne Francis	"	"		24	4	22	" "	"	"	"	Ditto	
472	"	"	"	Sherbourne Frank	"	"		12	7	23	" "	"	"	"	Ditto	
473	"	"	"	Sherbourne Fred	"	"		7	10	24		"	"	"	Ditto	
474	"	"	"	Breakspear Frederick Roy	Mr Breakspear	"		18	10	24		19	5	39	Age.	
475	"	"	"	Barnett Edward Stanley (~~William George~~)	Mr Wm G. Barnet	Kingston Lisle	—	17	4	20	~~Wm~~ Wincham Somerset.	31	7	30	Removed to Cheltenham	
476	"	"	"	Clanfield Dorothy	Mr A. Clanfield	West Challow.	—	12	9	24	NIL	27	4	33	To Farnham Pre Term.	See Page 18.
477	"	"	"	Holman Ruth	Mr F. Holman		—	2	9	24	NIL	8	11	29	To Appleford Wth Appleford C of E.	
363	9	9	29	Barry Norah	Mr J. Barry	West Challow.	—	29	7	20	Crescent Road Girls School Brist.	23	5	30	Driffield nr Cirencester Gloucester.	See Page 11 + 17
370	18	9	29	Tilley William	c/o Mr Wallington	Childrey	—	2	11	17	Little School Leaves.	↓	↓	↓	↓ (Tilley	See also Page 11 + 14.
478	22	10	29	Evans Ernest Claude	Mr Frank Evans	West Challow.	—	21	4	22	Grove.	20	5	36	Age. To Employment.	
431	28	10	29	Tomlin Hilda	Mr H. Tomlin	Childrey	—	15	9	22	Newton nr Tilbury	30	7	31	Attending School at [illegible] Wells during illness of mother	See also Pages 13 + 14.
479	7	1	30	Pointer Peter Alec	Mr W. Pointer	"	—	15	5	25	NIL	18	6	37	To Didcot	
480	"	"	"	Collingbourne Reg John	Mr R. Collingbourne	E. Challow.	—	12	1	25		31	7	30	Removed to Grove.	
481	"	"	"	Tomlin Frank Henry	Mr H. Tomlin	Childrey	—	26	3	25	"	30	7	31	Attending School at [illegible] Wells during illness of mother	
482	"	"	"	Hautin Joan Mary	Mr E. Hautin	"	—	31	1	25	"	6	10	39	Age. – To Employment.	
464	"	"	"	Rowland Dorothy Myra	Mr S. Rowland	Childrey	—	11	2	24	Bromley Hall Rd. School Abbott Rd. Poplar E. 14.	30	7	31	Attending School at Bromley Hall Rd. School Poplar E. 14.	See Also Page 14.
483	13	1	30	Morgan Verneuil	Mr Morgan	The Cabin Childrey	—	27	12	18	Charlton Kings Council Gloucestershire	12	6	31	Removed to Lambourne.	
392	13	1	30	Jacklin Dennis	c/o Mr G. Rowland	Childrey	—	3	9	21	Littleworth C of E. nr Faringdon	27	1	30	Returned to Littleworth	See Also Page 12
452	21	1	30	Jacklin Joyce	"	"	—	7	11	23	Littleworth C of E. nr Faringdon	28	1	30	Returned to Littleworth.	See Also Page 14
484	27	1	30	Gibbs Kenneth Edward	Mr A. Gibbs	East [illegible]	—	12	1		Clarence St. School Swindon	6	4	39	Age. To Employment.	
485	3	2	30	Webb Gwendoline	c/o Mrs Comley	High St. Childrey	—	24	8	27	Faringdon Council	14	2	30	Removed to [illegible]	
[illegible]	18	3	30	Shorter Harry	Mr H. A. Shorter	Church St.	—	20	5	24	East Challow.	24	9	31	To Hanney.	
487	1	4	30	Rowland Dennis A.B.	Mr S. Rowland	Stowell "	—	19	4	25	NIL	30	7	31	Attending School at	
488	"	"	"	Rowland Cyril John	Mr P. Rowland	West St. "	—	8	7	25	"	3	8	39	Age	
489	"	"	"	Arrowsmith Joyce	Mr W. Arrowsmith	C. Houses W. Challow	—	24	2	25	"	4	7	32	To The Grove. Wellington [illegible] Walk	
490	7	4	30	Legge Edward Henry	Mr Henry H. Legge.	5 " Childrey	—	5	2	25	"	3	11	39	Age. To Employment.	
491	29	4	30	Osborne Frederick Harold	Mr F. Osborne	High St. "	—	11	7	19	Southend South Church Council	31	7	30	Removed to an [illegible]	
492	"	"	"	Osborne Dorothy E.	"	"	—	31	1	17	"	"	"	"	"	
493	"	"	"	Osborne Joan	"	"	—	4	2	23	"	"	"	"	"	

Admission No. 16	Date of Admission (or Re-Admission) Day	Mon.	Year	Full Name of Child	Name of Parent or Guardian	Address	What Exemption, if any, from Religious Instruction is Claimed?	Date of Birth Day	Mon.	Year	Name of Last School	Date of Last Attendance at this School Day	Mon.	Year	Cause of Leaving	Remarks
494	29 (~~12~~)	4 (~~9~~)	30 (~~24~~)	Simmonds Leslie	Mr Reg. F. Simmonds	c/o Mr G. Rowland High St Childrey	None	12	9	24	On furlough from India	2	[illegible]	[illegible]	Father Returning to Regiment in India	
495	5	5	30	Osborne John Wilfred	Mr J. Osborne	Childrey	— "	28	5	21	Purleigh Council Essex	31	7	30	Removed to an address unknown	
496	12	5	30	Osborne David Thomas		"	— "	8	6	16	Purleigh Council Essex	31	7	30	Age	
370	7	7	30	Tilley William	c/o Mr Wallington	Childrey	— "	2	11	17	Driffield Glos.	23	12	31	Age	See also Pages 11 & 14 & 15
497	28	7	30	Sallows Maureen	Mr Sallows	Stowell "	—	24	3	23	Hindhead Council	28	11	30	To Highclere [illegible]	
498	8	9	30	Legge Helen Mary	Post Office Childrey	Mr H.C. Legge	— "	12	11	25	Nil	29	7	37	To Faringdon County School	
499	"	"	"	Hammond Ida Winnifred	High St "	Mr J Hammond	— "	29	9	25	Nil	22	12	39	Age.	
500	"	"	"	Hammond Edna Elsie	" "	"	— "	"	"	"	Nil	20	12	39	Age.	
501	"	"	"	Sheather Phyllis Rose	Hatchet Lane	[illegible] Sheather	"	21	10	25	Nil	22	12	39	Age.	
502	9	9	30	Barnett Ormond Cecil [illegible]	Blowing Stone Cottages	Mr Wm G. Barnett	"	31	11	23	Kingston Lisle	1	6	31	To Mrs. Atkins' (~~[illegible]~~) Private School Wantage	
503	15	9	30	Pembro Joan	The Bakery Childrey	Mr H.R. Pembro	"	17	4	24	Cross Keys Newport	30	3	31	Returned to Cross Keys	
504	29	9	30	Green Pearl	Holme Lea West Challow	[illegible]	— "	[illegible]	[illegible]	[illegible]	Mrs Shepherd's Private Twyford	3	[illegible]	31	Removed from District Tewkesbury Glos.?	
5045	6	11	30	Harris Ruth	West St Childrey	Mr Jas Harris	— "	27	10	21	Alvechurch Nr Birmingham	3	8	34	Removed to Poole.	
506	"	"	"	Harris John Thomas	" " "	" "	— "	22	4	23	"	3	8	34	Removed to Poole	
507	"	"	"	Harris Isaac	" " "	" "	— "	7	9	25	"	3	8	34	Removed to Poole.	
508	8	12	30	Webdale (Webdell) ~~George~~ John Frederick	Stowell "	Mr Fred ~~Webdale~~ Web	— "	4	3	24	Wanborough Nr Swindon				[illegible]	
509	"	"	"	~~Webdale~~ Webdell Barbara Grace	" "	" " "	— "	31	8	21	" "				[illegible]	
404	15	12	30	Tilley Marjorie	Mrs Tilley	c/o Mr Wallington Childrey	—	28	1	21	Alvescote Children's Home School Nr Oxford	24	11	33	Admitted to Cottage Homes Wallingford & attending Wallingford C of E Girls	See also Page 12 & 14.
510	6	1	31	Hunt Marion [illegible]	Mr E. Hunt	[illegible]	—	9	1	26	[illegible]	14	10	31	Removed to East Challow	
511	"	"	"	Peke Rodney Leonard William	Mr R Peke		—	18	1	26	"	21	3	40	Age.	
512	"	"	"	Allsopp [illegible]	Mr R. Allsopp		—	[illegible]	[illegible]	[illegible]		5 (~~27~~)	5 (~~4~~)	40 (~~40~~)	Age – To Employment (~~Age.~~)	
513	"	"	"	Comley Florence	Mr C. Comley	High St "	—	[illegible]	1	26	"	21	3	40	Age.	
514	"	"	"	Collett Helen Rosena Cecilia	Mr C. Collett			31	10	25		5	10	33	To Grove Pro Tem. Illness of Mother	See Page 18 & 20
515	"	"	"	Waring Nonna Marjorie	c/o Mr E. Froud	Pond [illegible]		[illegible]	[illegible]	[illegible]	Rosendale Rd. Herne Hill	5	2	31	Returned Home to London	
497	23	2	31	Sallows Maureen	Mr Sallows	Stow Hill Childrey		24	3	23	No school attended while away – Unwell.	24	3	32	Removed to Grove, Berks	
516	1	4	31	Gregory Albert John	Mr Alfred Gregory	Corn Hill [illegible]		24	2	19	East Challow.	31	3	33	Age.	
517	1	4	31	Gregory Arthur Sidney		"		12	5	20	" "	3	5	34	Age.	
518	"	"	"	Green Lawrence Arthur	Mr J. Green	Childrey		19	4	26	Nil	28	10	37	Removed to Blewbury.	
519	"	"	"	Barry Michael John	Mr J. Barry	West Challow.		30	5	26	Nil.	31	7	40	Age.	
520	"	"	"	Matthews George Collins	Mr G. Matthews	Lodge Farm Childrey		29	1	26	Nil	29	1	37	To King Alfred's School Wantage.	
521	"	"	"	Bungay Phyllis Mary	Mr W. Bungay	Chapel Cottages		23	7	26	Nil.	31	7	40	Age.	
522	"	"	"	Pointer Phyllis	Mr W. Pointer	Council Houses Childrey		14	5	26.	Nil	18	6	37	To Didcot	
523	14	4	31	Mepstead Jean Evelyn	Mr H. W. Mepstead	c/o Mr J. Hammond [illegible]		31	3	26	Nil.	5	5	31	Removed [illegible]	
524	4	5	31	Law Peter John Victor	c/o Mrs Burls	Stow Hill, Childrey			2	25	Lambourne C of E	21	7	39	To Employment Age.	
525	11 (~~[illegible]~~)	5	31	Bailey James William	c/o Mrs Bennett	Hatchet Lane	—	28	5	26	Nil	7	10	31	To Radnor Road Faringdon	
526	20	7	31	Atkins Amelia Lily	Collins Wilfred Albert Mokeking (Stepfather)	The Cabin	—	15	6	25	Broadbrook Bracknell.	3	8	39	Age.	

16

Admission No. 17	Date of Admission (or Re-Admission) Day	Mon.	Year	Full Name of Child	Name of Parent or Guardian	Address	What Exemption, if any, from Religious Instruction is Claimed?	Date of Birth Day	Mon.	Year	Name of Last School	Date of Last Attendance at this School Day	Mon.	Year	Cause of Leaving	Remarks 11 17
459	7	9	31	Burton Evelyn Annie	Mr G. Burton	West St. Childrey	—	21	3	23	Readmitted from Kenilworth School near Leamington Warwick	23	12	31	To Miss Aitkin's School Wantage as Boarder	
527	21	9	31	Gregory William Victor	Mr A. Gregory	Corn Hill West Challow	—	3	1	23	East Challow	4	10	36	Left District Removed to Shipton under Wychwood	
528	"	"	"	Newman Thomas	Mr F. Newman	West St. Childrey	—	23	1	17	Letcombe Bassett	25	5	32	To East Challow	
529	"	"	"	Newman John Edward	"	"	—	2	6	21	" "	"	"	"	" "	
530	21	9	31	Gibbs Alan Stanley	Mr A. Gibbs	East Manton Stalls	—	22	9	26	—	17	1	41	Age – To Employment	
431	21	9	31	Tomlin Hilda	Mr H. Tomlin	High St. Childrey	—	15	9	22	Blunsdon Wilts	20	11	31	To Blunsdon Wilts for Term	See Pages 13. 14 and 15
481	"	"	"	Tomlin Frank Henry	"	"	—	26	3	25	Blunsdon Wilts	6	4	39	Age. For employment	See Page 15
531	7	1	32	James Albert Robert	Mr J. James	Stow Hill	—	5	11	24	Convent St Helens Southsea the Seaford (Thanet)	4	11	34	To Kingston on Thames	
532	"	"	"	James Evelyn Joan	"	"	—	"	"	"	"	4	11	34	To Kingston on Thames	
533	"	"	"	Rowland Eric Roy	Mr P. Rowland	West St.	—	9	1	27	Nil	10	4	41	Age	
534	"	"	"	Pike Ernest Roy	Mr R. Pike	Stow Hill	—	3	2	27	Nil	1	6	32	Deceased	
535	"	"	"	Clanfield Edith Rose	Mr A. Clanfield	West Challow	—	20	4	26	Nil	20	12	40	Age	
464	"	"	"	Rowland Dorothy Myra	Mr S. Rowland	Stow Hill Childrey	—	11	2	24	Bromley Hall Rd. School	25	3	38	Age	See Pages 14 & 15. Absent three weeks before leaving
487	18	1	32	Rowland Dennis A.B.	"		—	19	4	25	Market Rd. School East Ham Upton Park	3	8	39	Age	See Page 15
536	25	1	32	Booker Vaughan	Mr V. Booker	Council Houses Sparsholt	—	11	5	26	—	19	3	34	Removed from Register as unfit to attend school. Certificate by Local Authority 19.3.34 under Sec. 10(b) of Educ. Act 1921 (Age)	
537	~~30~~	~~7~~	~~26~~	Law Dorothy Edna	Mr W. Law	High St. Childrey	—	30	7	26	Nil	19	6	40	Age. Excluded Measles 19-6-40 – 31-7-40.	
538	4	4	32	Lester Gladys Ellen	Mr G. Lester	Council Houses W. Challow	—	14	5	27	Nil	19	12	41	Age.	
431	4	4	32	Tomlin Hilda	Mr H. Tomlin	High St. Childrey	—	15	9	22	Blunsdon Wilts	23	12	36	Age.	See above & Pages 13. 14 & 15
539	13 ~~25~~	6 ~~7~~	32 ~~26~~	Alexander Kathleen Mary	Mr H. Alexander	c/o Miss Sharp, Old Manor West St. Childrey	—	25	7	26		3	9	36	Removed to Wendover Bucks (c/o Miss Sharp)	Attending Wendover C of E.
540	5	9	32	Mays Kenneth Arthur	Mr F. Mays	c/o Mr Pilliger Childrey	—	16	8	26	Boxgrove C of E nr Chichester	1	6	33	To Kingston Lisle	
541	"	"	"	Gregory Leslie Walter	Mr A. Gregory	Corn Hill	—	2	4	25	East Challow C of E	9	10	36	Removed to Shipton under Wychwood.	
542	"	"	"	Marchant Queenie Nevill Adoree	Mrs W. Marchant	Stow Hill	—	7	12	27	—	19	12	41	Age.	
543	12	9	32	Hamilton Ernest George	Mr G. H. Hamilton	~~Hamleigh~~ Holmlea West Challow	—	6	4	25	Abbots Ann nr Andover	10	3	37	Removed to Hanney	
544	"	"	"	Hamilton Jean Margaret	"	"	—	5	5	27	"	10	3	37	Removed to Hanney	
545	4	10	32	Clements Dorothy	c/o Mr Clements	Dog Lane Childrey	—	28	7	26	Highworth Wilts	-	10	32	Returned to Highworth.	
546	9	1	33	Gregory Frank Thomas	Mr A. Gregory	Corn Hill	—	14	8	28	—	9	10	36	Removed to Shipton under Wychwood	
547	"	"	"	Rowland Ivor Vivian	Mr S. Rowland	Council Houses Childrey	—	3	12	27	—	19	12	41	Age.	
548	"	"	"	Davey Robert Paul	c/o Mrs A. Froud	The Hatchet Childrey	—	25	4	25	Lochmaben nr Dumfries Scotland	31	3	33	Returned to Lochmaben	
549	"	"	"	Gregory Gwendoline Flora	Mr A. Gregory	Corn Hill Childrey	—	17	6	24	East Challow	9	10	36	Removed to Shipton under Wychwood.	
550	1	2	33	Ellis Frederick Francis	Mr F. Ellis	c/o Mr Marchant	—	15	1	26	Loch Maben Dumfriesshire Scotland	31	3	33	Returned to Lochmaben	See also Page 19
551	"	"	"	Ellis Jean Mary	"	"	—	12	9	27	"	31	3	33	" "	
363	20	2	33	Barry Norah	Mr J. Barry	West Challow	—	24	7	20	Present Rd. Erith	7	8	34	Age. Employment.	See also Pages 1. 5 & 11
552	1	3	33	Harrolds Pamela	Mr J. Harrolds	West St. Childrey	—	29	12	27	Sparsholt C of E	22	11	33	To Relatives at Bicester Oxford – then to be attending School	
553	15	3	33	Males Henry Cyril	Mr Paul Males	The Forge Childrey	—	25	6	19	St Marys Hall Lindley & previously Ketton Derby	4	8	33	Left for Work – Age.	
554	3	4	33	Saunders Norman Geoffrey	Mr W. Saunders	Childrey Warren	—	3	8	19	Letcombe Bassett	4	8	33	Left for Work. – Age.	
555	"	"	"	McCaig John	Mr J. McCaig	Sparsholt	—	4	5	20	Sparsholt C of E	3	5	34	Age. – Work.	

Admission No.	Date of Admission (or Re-Admission) Day	Mon.	Year	Full Name of Child	Name of Parent or Guardian	Address	What Exemption, if any, from Religious Instruction is Claimed?	Date of Birth Day	Mon.	Year	Name of Last School	Date of Last Attendance at this School Day	Mon.	Year	Cause of Leaving	Remarks
556	3	4	33	Williams Stanley	Mr H. Williams	Cowleaze Childrey	—	5	2	21	Letcombe Bassett	1	2	35	Removed to Caswell Marsh. Admitted Littleworth C of E	
557	"	"	"	McCaig Benjamin	Mr J. McCaig	Sparsholt	—	6	6	25	Sparsholt	3	8	39	Age.	
558	"	"	"	McCaig Robert	"	"	—	21	2	27	"	"	"	"	To Sparsholt C of E.	
559	"	"	"	McCaig Alan	"	"	—	17	5	28	"	"	"	"	To Sparsholt C of E.	
560	"	"	"	McCaig Annie	"	"	—	6	12	21	"	18	12	35	Age.	
561	"	"	"	McCaig Mary	"	"	—	23	12	22	"	23	12	36	Age.	
562	"	"	"	Collett Francis Marjorie	Mr C. Collett	West Challow	—	10	5	28	None	5	10	33	To Grove for Time Illness of Mother	
563	"	"	"	Alder Ivy Patience	Mr J. Alder	High St. Childrey	—	26	11	28	"	13	8	42	Age	
564	"	"	"	Alder Iris Joyce	"	"	—	"	"	"	"	13	8	42	Age.	
565	"	"	"	Matthews Kathleen Lillian	Mr G. Matthews	Lodge Farm Childrey	—	11	5	28	"	19	1	37	To Faringdon County School	
566	4	4	33	Bull Mary Irene Thelma	Mr C. Bull	Church St. "	—	23	6	28	"	13	2	42	Age	
567	25	4	33	Sims William John Cattell	Mr C. Sims	Elm Tree Cottage "	—	14	2	27	Vamber End. Basingstoke	[illegible]	11	34	To Cardiff	
568	"	"	"	Sims Vera Catherine	"	"	—	30	6	22	" "	[illegible]	11	34	To Cardiff	
569	15	5	33	Dance Peter Charles Mary	c/o Mr G. Dance	West St. Childrey	—	6	6	27	Hanney C of E	4	7	33	Returned to Hanney.	See P. 20.
570				Uzzell Eileen Pamela	c/o Mr R. Evans	West Challow.	—	10	1	25	Alfred Sutton Reading	4	7	33	Returned to Reading	Travelling Theatre Company
571	18	7	33	Armstrong Pearl	Mrs Armstrong	c/o Mrs Rowland [illegible] c/o Mrs Brooks [illegible]	—	13	5	24	Stanford in Vale.	-	-	-	To East Hendred	" "
571	"	"	"	Armstrong Ada Mavis Fern		"	—	17	5	25	" "	-	-	-	To East Hendred.	
572	11	9	33	Evans Pearl Maude	Mr A. Evans	West [illegible]	—	21	2	27	Wantage C of E	9	4	36	To Wantage C of E	
573	"	"	"	Williams Lillian Lilly	Mr H. Williams	Cowleaze	—	23	4	22	Letcombe Bassett	1	2	35	Removed to Caswell Marsh Admitted Littleworth C of E	
574				Weddell Patricia Elizabeth	Mr F.G. Weddell	C. Houses Childrey	—	25	3	28	—				" "	
575	"	"	"	Gibbs Barbara Joyce	Mr A. Gibbs	East Hanton	—	5	8	28	—	13	8	42	Age.	
476	"	"	"	Clanfield Dorothy May	Mrs A. Clanfield	West Challow	—	12	9	24	Fernham C of E.	23	12	38	Age.	See Also Page 15
404	21	9	33	Tilley Marjorie	Mrs Tilley	c/o Mr Wallington Woodline Cottage. Childrey	—	27	1	22	Wallingford C of E.	18	5	34	Removed to "The Severals" Marlborough. Attending Milton Lilbourne School.	Returned from College Farm Wallingford. See Pages 12 and 16
552	29	1	34	Harolds Pamela	Mr J. Harolds	West St. Childrey	—	29	12	27	Bicester C of E Senior School Oxon.	[illegible]	[illegible]	[illegible]	To Bicester for [illegible]	Attended Bicester 13-11-33 - 25-1-34 See Below. (See Page 17)
576	8	1	34	Law Barbara Violet	Mr A.V. Law	Stow Lane Childrey	—	8	12	28	None	4	12	42	Removed to Wantage To Wantage C of E.	
577	"	"	"	Rowland Kathleen Margaret ~~Katherine~~	Mr P. Rowland	West St. Childrey	—	29	12	28	"	23	12	42	Age.	
578	"	"	"	Bennett Joyce	Mr R. Bennett.	Stow Hill Childrey	—	18	2	29	"	22	4	43	Age	
579	7	2	34	Christian Robert Keith	Mrs Alethea Christian	c/o Rev. Sheppard - The Rectory Childrey	—	8	5	23	Curdridge Council nr Southampton	30	10	34	Left District.	
514	9	4	34	Collett Celia Joyce Rosina	Mr C. Collett.	West Challow	—	31	10	25	Returned from Grove	19	6	36.	To Grandmother at Grove for Time. Attending School there	See Also Page 16 - 20
580	"	"	"	Stratton Violet Mary	Mrs [illegible] Stratton	West Challow		[illegible]	[illegible]	29	None	22	4	43	Age.	
581	"	"	"	Haines Brian William Henry	Mr F.J. Haines	"		28	6	29	"	22	11	35	To Stanford-in-the-Vale for time	
562	16	4	34	Collett Francis [illegible]	Mr C. Collett	" "	—	[illegible]			Grove C.P.	21	12	39	To Wantage C of E.	See [illegible] Same Age
404	9	7	34	Tilley Marjorie	c/o Mr R. Wallington	Woodline Cottage Childrey	—	27	1	21	Milton Lilbourne nr Marlborough.	18	4	35	Age	See Above & pages 12 & 16
582	10	9	34	Tomlin Iris Doreen	Mr H. Tomlin	High St. Childrey	—	1	12	29	—	12	6	36	Away from Home for Time. Attending School at Stratton	
540	"	"	"	Mays Kenneth	Mr F. Mays	c/o Mrs Pellefer. Stow Hill Childrey.	—	16	5	26	Kingston Lisle	10	12	40	Age. To Employment.	See Page [illegible]
552	[illegible]	7	34	Harolds Pamela	Mr J. Harolds	West St. Childrey	—	19	12	27	Bicester C of E.	9	11	34	To Bicester for Time	See Page 17 [illegible] Above

19

Admission No.	Date of Admission (or Re-Admission) Day	Mon.	Year	Full Name of Child	Name of Parent or Guardian	Address	What Exemption, if any, from Religious Instruction is Claimed?	Date of Birth Day	Mon.	Year	Name of Last School	Date of Last Attendance at this School Day	Mon.	Year	Cause of Leaving	Remarks
583	10	9	34	Williams Richard	Mr H. Williams	Cowleaze Childrey	—	23	4	27	Letcombe Bassett	24	1	35	Removed to Carswell Marsh. Admitted Littleworth C of E.	
584	"	"	"	Williams Edith	Ditto	Ditto	—	1	2	25	Ditto	1	2	35	Removed to Carswell Marsh Admitted Littleworth C of E.	
585	"	"	"	Rowland Peggy Ellen	Mr W. Rowland	Council Houses Childrey	—	20	10	29	NIL	13	12	40	To West Ilsley.	
✓ 586	"	"	"	Legge Douglas	Mr H. Legge	" " "	—	21	8	29	"	12	8	43	Age – Summer Holiday	
587	"	"	"	Rowland June Agnes Pamela	Mr S. Rowland	" "	—	16	7	29	NIL	30	7	43	Age.	
588	"	"	"	Booker Alfreda June	Mr V. Booker	" "	—	3	6	29	NIL	30	7	43	Age.	
589	"	"	"	McCaig Irene Elsie	Mr J. McCaig	Sparsholt	—	7	9	29	NIL	3	8	39	To Sparsholt C of E.	
✓ 590	"	"	"	Barry Ernest Leslie	Mr J. Barry	West Challow	—	2	9	29	NIL	26	5	43	Age in Summer Holiday Excluded until then with Ringworm.	
523	17	9	34	Mepstead Jean Evelyn	Mr H. W. Mepstead	c/o Mrs J. Hammond West St Childrey	—	31	3	26	Rochester	27	9	34	Returned to Rochester	
591	18	9	34	Brookes Alan Alfred	Mr Alfred Edward Brookes	Godfrey's Farm Cottage Childrey	—	1	7	29	NIL	12 / 24	7	35 / 35	To St Lukes C of E Tonbridge Wells	See Below
✓ 592	24	9	34	Bedford Phyllis Mary	Mr E. Bedford	West Challow	—	24	8	29	NIL	12	8	43	Age in Summer Holiday	
593	18	9	34	Giles Robert	Mr G. H. Giles	Dog Lane Childrey	—	8	8	28		7	8	42	Age.	
552	19	11	34	Harolds Pamela	Mr J. Harolds	West St. Childrey	—	29	12	27	Grecester C of E	15	4	35	To Grecester	See Pages 17 and 18 (…)
567	7	1	35	Sims John Cottrell	Mrs E Sims	Herman's Terrace Childrey	—	19	2	27	Cardiff?	10	4	41	Age.	
568	"	"	"	Sims Vera Catherine	"	" " "	—	30	6	22	Cardiff!	30	7	36.	Age.	
✓ 594	"	"	"	Ellwood Frederick Thomas	Mr F. Ellwood	West Challow	—	12	10	29	None	24	12	43	Age.	
✓ 595	"	"	"	Sheather John	Mr J. Sheather	C. Houses Childrey	—	19	2	30	None	6	4	44	Age.	
* 596.	22	10	34	Mason Helen Margaret Alice	Mr J. Mason	Greendown Farm "	—	14	2	21	North Fawley	17	4	35	Age.	* Entry overlooked at time hence number not in true sequence.
* 597	"	"	"	Mason Ernest George		" "	—	8	5	24	"	17	4	35	To Letcombe Regis School.	
✓ 598	29	4	35	Rowland Albert John	Mr J. Rowland	West St. Childrey	—	27	5	30	NONE	31	7	44	Age.	
✓ 599	"	"	"	Bungay Alan	Mr W. Bungay	Council Houses "	—	17	1	30	NONE	6	4	47	Age.	
✓ 600	"	"	"	Young Mary	Mr F. Young	Stow Hill Childrey	—	29	4	30	NONE	23	2	43.	To Wantage C of E Girls (…)	
601	"	"	"	Hamilton Sheila Mary	Mr G. H. Hamilton	West Challow	Roman Catholic	24	3	30	NONE	29	4	36.	To Andover. Attending Weyhill Street Council Infants – Andover.	Father fatally injured in an cycle accident. Child away with grandmother.
602	"	"	"	Costello Bridget	Mr J. Costello	West Challow	Roman Catholic	18	4	28	Kingston Lisle	13	9	35.	Removed to Eastbury nr. Lambourne.	
550	1	5	35	Ellis Frederick Francis	Mr F. Ellis	c/o Mrs Marchant Stow Hill.	NIL	15	1	26	Dumfries Lochmaben Public School	21 / 8	3 / 8	40 / 39	Age.	See Also Page 17
551	"	"	"	Ellis Jean Mary	"	" "	"	12	6	27	Ditto	31	7	41	Age.	
552	8	5	35	Harolds Pamela	Mr J. Harolds	West St. Childrey	"	29	12	27	To Grecester	19	6	35	To Grecester C of E (…)	See Also Pages 17 & 18 (…)
603	7	6	35	Windridge Raymond Peter	Mr E. W. Windridge	High St. Childrey	"	13	9	28	Denchworth.	3	7	36	To Wantage. – Attending C of E. School.	
591	9	9	35	Brookes Alan Alfred	Mr A. Brookes.	Godfreys Farm Cottage	NIL	1	9	29	St Lukes C of E Tonbridge Wells	19	1	37.	To Tonbridge Wells (…) attending St. Lukes C of E.	See Above.
604	19 / 19	9 / X	35 / 26	Rawlings Joan Elizabeth	Mr F. Rawlings	c/o Mrs Bullmore, West St. Childrey	NIL	9	5	26	Ferndale Road Swindon	3	12	35	Removed to 3 Hill Farm Cottages, (…) Town Hill	S Kelly, Swansea.
✓ 605	"	"	"	Rowland Pamela Elsie Joan	Mr P. Rowland	West St. Childrey	NIL	17	12	30	NONE	18	5	45	Age. To Employment	
606	"	"	"	Pointer Beryl	Mr W. Pointer	C. Houses "	NIL	25	10	30	NONE	18	6	37	To Didcot	
607	"	"	"	Evans Christine Anne	Mr R Evans	West Challow	"	29	10	30	NONE	15	10	36.	Removed to Kirkland (…) attending East Challow School because of distance.	
✓ 608	"	"	"	Law Pamela Nelly	Mr A. V. Law	Stow Hill Childrey	"	27	9	30	NONE	4	12	42	Removed to Wantage To Wantage C of E.	
✓ 609	"	"	"	Lester Philip Charles	Mr C. Lester	C. Houses W. Challow	"	9	11	30	NONE	18	5	45	Age To Employment	
610	"	"	"	Pike Kenneth Arthur	Mr R. Pike	Stow Hill Childrey	"	11	12	30	NONE	21	3	40	To East Challow	
611	"	"	"	Rawlings Kenneth Hugh		c/o Mrs Bullmore West St. Childrey	"	3	3	29	Ferndale Rd Swindon	3	12	35	See No. 604 above.	

Admission No. 20	Date of Admission (or Re-Admission) Day	Mon.	Year	Full Name of Child	Name of Parent or Guardian	Address	What Exemption, if any, from Religious Instruction, is Claimed?	Date of Birth Day	Mon.	Year	Name of Last School	Date of Last Attendance at this School Day	Mon.	Year	Cause of Leaving	Remarks 20
612	9	9	35	Haines Basil	Mr F. J. Haines	West Challow	NONE	5	9	30	NONE	21	11	35	To Stanford-in-the-Vale Pro Tem.	
613	"	"	"	Allison Cyril	Mr Allison	"	"	21	3	28	Private School Richmond Hants	30	7	36	To Swindon attending Clarence St. Boys.	
548	2	10	35	Davey Robert Paul	c/o Mrs Froud	The Hatchet Childrey	"	25	4	25	Norton Council Boys Malton Yorks	4	10	35	Returned to Malton	See also Page 17
614	6	1	36	Pottinger Linda Joy	Mr E. Pottinger	C. Houses Childrey	"	30	3	31	None	20	3	36	To Stanford in Vale (Return)	
✓ 615	"	"	"	Giles Janet	Mr G. Giles	West St. "	"	27	2	31	None.	29	3	45	Age.	
616	"	"	"	Breakspear Roland	Mr J. Breakspear	c/o Mrs Welch Stow Hill	"	19	8	30	Blunsdon Wilts	10	1	36	To Shrivenham	See Below.
581	"	"	"	Haines Brian	Mr F. J. Haines	West Challow	"	28	6	29	Stanford-in-Vale	17	10	41	To Gt Coxwell School	See Page 18
612	9	"	"	Haines Basil	"	" "	"	5	9	30	" " "	19	3	36	Admitted to Peppard Sanatorium School.	See above & Log Book
616	3	2	36	Breakspear Rowland	Mr J. Breakspear	c/o Mrs Bennett Stow Hill	"	19	8	30	From Shrivenham	12	3	36	To Goosey & attending School there.	See above
569	"	"	"	Dance Peter Charles	c/o Mrs G. Dance	West St. Childrey	"	6	6	27	East Hanney	9	4	36	Returned to Hanney.	See Page 18
617	5	3	36.	~~Dance~~ Edwards Eliz Alice Mary	c/o Mrs S. Taylor	High St. Childrey	"	22	3	30	" "	12	3	36.	Returned to Hanney.	
✓ 618	21	4	36	Epwood Frederick	Mr G. Epwood	Council Houses	"	20	5	31	None	20	7	45	Age	
✓ 619	"	"	"	Stratton Robert Thomas.	Mr R. Stratton	West Challow.	"	11	5	31	None	26	7	43	Age.	
620	11	5	36	Cook William Thomas	Mr Edward Thomas Cook	West Challow	"	5	7	25	Wantage Council.	19	6	36	Away from Home Pro Tem attending School at Cadley Nr Marlborough.	Notification sent by parent
622	"	"	"	Cook Frederick Charles	" " "	" "	"	5	3	30	"	19	6	36.		
✓ 616	9	3	36	Breakspear Rowland	Mr J. Breakspear	Stow Hill Childrey	None	19	8	30.	Goosey.	10	8	44	Age.	See Above (Two Entries)
Above * 620	27	4	36	Pickup Elizabeth Ellen	c/o Mrs Harolds	High St. Childrey	None.	18	10	28	Bicester	19	6	36.	Returned to Bicester	
614	6	1	36	Pottinger Linda Joy	Mr E. Pottinger	Council Houses Childrey	"	30	3	31	Stanford in the Vale	10	1	38	To Stanford in the Vale Pro tem.	See Above
621	29	6	36	Cook William Thomas	Mr Edward T. Cook	West Challow	"	5	7	25	Cadley Nr Marlborough.	14	10	36	Deceased.	See Above. [illegible]
622	29	7	36	Cook Frederick Charles	" "	" "	"	5	3	30	"	20	3	39	Removed to Lyford?	See above & as brother
552	29	7	35	Harolds Pamela	Mr J. Harolds	High St. Childrey	"	29	12	27.	Bicester	7	5	37	To Letcombe Regis	See also Pages 17, 18 and 19 (Twice)
514	1	9	36.	Collett Helga Rosena Celia	Mr C. Collett	West Challow	"	31	10	25	Grove.	18	11	38	To Grove with Grandparents attending School Wantage	See also Pages 16 and 18
601	"	"	"	Hamilton Sheila Mary	Mrs G. H. Hamilton	" "	Exemption claimed Roman Catholic	24	3	30.	Newbury St. Council Infants Andover	10	3	37	Removed to Hanney	See Page 19
623	1	9	36	Goatley Patricia Emma Doreen	c/o Mrs Males.	The Forge High St. Childrey	None	3	9	27	Fawley.	29	1	37	Returned Fawley	
548	28	9	36	Davey Robert Paul	c/o Mrs O. Froud	The Hatchet Childrey	None	25	4	25	Norton Council School Malton Yorks	2	10	36.	Returned to Malton Yorks	
✓ 582	1	10	36	Tomlin Iris	Mr H. Tomlin	High St. Childrey	None	1	12	29	Upper Stratton Nr Swindon	20	12	43	Age.	See also Page 18. Not School since May 1935 until date of admission
624	12	1	37	Hicks Graham Arthur Clement	Mr John R. Hicks	Sincombe Farm Childrey	None.	26	11	29	Kingston Lisle	28	9	37	Left District	
✓ 625	6	4	37	Ellis June	Mr F. Ellis	Stow Hill Childrey	None	12	6	32	None	30	7	46	Age - To Employment.	
626	"	"	"	Pottinger Ruth	Mr E. Pottinger	Council Houses	None	26	6	32	None	14	1	38.	To Stanford in the Vale (pro tem)	
✓ 627	"	"	"	Sheather Ronald	Mr J. Sheather	" "	None	7	7	32	None	31	7	46.	Age.	
628	"	"	"	Jepson Brenda Maud	Mrs Harold Jepson.	West Challow	None.	21	1	32	None	28	6	38	Removed to Sparsholt.	
✓ 612	"	"	"	Haines Basil	Mr J. Haines	West Challow	None	5	9	30	Peppard Sanatorium	21	12	44	Age.	See above same page.
591	"	"	"	Brooks Alan	Mr A. Brooks	Goosey [illegible]		1	3	[illegible]	St. Lukes [illegible]	1	5	38	Removed to Didcot.	See also Page [illegible]
629	14	4	37	Barber William Ernest	Mr W. R. Barber	Mayo Farm Cottage W. Challow		8	6	26	Aldworth	11	5	37	Left District? Watchfield	
630	4	5	37	Pearman Herbert Henry	Mr G. Pearman	Box Cottage West Challow	None	29	1	29		29	7	37	Left District?	Admitted [illegible] School.

| Admission No. 21 | Date of Admission Day | Mon. | Year | Full Name of Child | Name of Parent or Guardian | Address | What Exemption, if any, from Religious Instruction, is Claimed? | Date of Birth Day | Mon. | Year | Name of Last School | Date of Last Attendance at this School Day | Mon. | Year | Cause of Leaving | Remarks | 21
|---|---|---|---|---|---|---|---|---|---|---|---|---|---|---|---|---|
| 631 | 24 | 5 | 37 | ~~Cousins~~ Cozens Harry James | Mr E. Cousins | The Manor House Childrey | Nil | 3 | 6 | 26 | Norfolk Haveringland School | 20 | 1 | 39 | Left District | |
| 632 | " | " | " | Wood Robert | Mr Frederick Wood | c/o Mrs Legge Post Office Childrey | Nil | 30 | 8 | 31 | East Farley Kent | 18 | 6 | 37 | Returned to East Farley | |
| 633 | 12 ~~20~~ | 7 | 37 | Curtis Violet | c/o Mr King | Manor Gardens Cottage | Nil | 26 | 1 | 31 | Eastlands, Rugby | 4 | 7 | 37 | Returned to Eastlands Rugby | {Absent 12-7-37 – 29-7-37 With Scarlet Fever} |
| 634 | " | " | " | Curtis Edith Lucy | | " " | None | 16 | 4 | 29 | | 29 | 7 | 37 | Returned to Eastlands Rugby | |
| ✓ 635 | 6 | 9 | 37 | Bedford Merlyn | Mr E. Bedford | Council Houses West Challow | None | 1 | 9 | 32 | None | 3 | 7 | 46 | Age. – To Employment | |
| 539 | 6 ~~[illegible]~~ | 9 | 37 | Alexander Kathleen Mary | Mrs H. Alexander | Old Vicarage West Challow | None | 25 | 7 | 26 | Wendover Bucks | 17 | 2 | 39 | To Miss Adkin Private School, Wantage | See Pages 17 – |
| 636 | 13 | 9 | 37 | Ellbro June May | Mr Joseph Charles Ellbro | West St. Childrey | None | 27 | 1 | 30 | Ashbury | 19 | 9 | 38 | To Foxhill – c/o Mr Barker – Foxhill | |
| 638 | 4 | 10 | 37 | Burns Jean | c/o Mrs Lewis | Chapel Cottages, Childrey | None | 23 | 2 | 31 | Council School Hornchurch | 15 | 10 | 37 | Returned Hornchurch | Board Gurneys Hornchurch Essex Mrs Burns 36 Glebe Way |
| 637 | 20 | 9 | 37 | Fathers Marie | c/o Mrs G. Embling | West St. Childrey | None | 9 | 12 | 32 | None | 8 | 4 | 37 | Removed to Steventon | Removed to Steventon |
| 638 | 12 | 10 | 37 | Coles Irene Mabel | Mr Coles | West Challow | None | 20 | 2 | 25 | Chilton Foliat | 19 | 11 | 37 | Removed to Bishopstone nr Swindon | |
| 639 | " | " | " | Coles Ernest Alfred | " | " | " | 17 | 10 | 29 | Chilton Foliat | 18 | 11 | 37 | | |
| 640 | 13 | 12 | 37 | Johnson Edward George | Mr William " | West Challow | None | 18 | 2 | 26 | Burford | 20 | 9 | 38 | To Casual Ward & then to Inst. Bampton, Oxon | Temp. Adm. Woodstock for Inst. [illegible] |
| 641 | 13 | 12 | 37 | Johnson Leonard | " " | " " | " | 15 | 8 | 27 | Burford | " | " | " | " | |
| 642 | 13 | 12 | 37 | Johnson William James | " " | " " | " | 20 | 1 | 31 | Burford | " | " | " | " | |
| ✓ 643 | 5 | 1 | 38 | Tomlin Daphne Joan | Mr H. Tomlin | High St. Childrey | None | 29 | 12 | 32 | None | 18 | 12 | 46 | Age. To Employment | |
| ✓ 644 | 5 | 1 | 38 | Haines Rosemary Dawn | Mrs F. Haines | 1 Council Houses, West Challow | None | 16 | 2 | 33 | None | 17 | 2 | 47 | Age. To Employment. | School closed – lack of fuel 10/2–17-2-47 – Fuel |
| ✓ 645 | 5 | 1 | 38 | Cox Keith Thomas Vaughan | Mr T. Cox | Council Houses W. Challow | None | 28 | 12 | 32 | None | 25 | 4 | 47 | Age To Employment | |
| 597 | 17 | 1 | 38 | Mason Ernest George | Mr J. Mason | Greendown Farm, Childrey | None | 8 | 11 | 24 | Letcombe Regis | 20 | 12 | 38 | Age | Also Page 19 |
| 614 | 2 | 2 | 38 | Pottinger Linda Joy | Mr E. Pottinger | Council Houses, Childrey | " " | 30 | 3 | 31 | Stanford | 29 | 3 | 39 | To Stanford-in-Vale (Pottinger) | } Also Page 20 |
| 626 | 14 | 2 | 38 | Pottinger Ruth | Mr E. Pottinger | Council Houses, Childrey | — | 26 | 6 | 32 | Stanford | 4 | 3 | 39 | To Stanford-in-Vale (Pottinger) | } |
| ✓ 646 | 22 ~~21~~ | 2 ~~3~~ | 38 ~~29~~ | Rea Robert | Mr Percy Rea | 'Dropshort' Cress Beds | | 21 | 11 | 28 ~~29~~ | Cold Ash Hospital | 23 | 12 | 42 | Age | ½ day only (M.O) |
| | 26 ~~[illegible]~~ | 4 | 38 | ~~West Robert~~ | | Childrey Berks | | | | | | – | – | – | | |
| 632 | 26 | 4 | 38 | Wood Robert | Mr Wood | c/o Post Office Childrey | — | 30 | 8 | 31 | St Margaret's at Cliff Dover | 15 | 5 | 38 | Returned to St Margaret's Bay | Also Above |
| ~~[illegible]~~ 650 | ~~[illegible]~~ 2 | ~~[illegible]~~ 5 | ~~[illegible]~~ 38 | Collins Dorothy | Mr P. Collins | Stowell Childrey | — | 27 | 4 | 33 | None | 4 | 3 | 41 | To Didcot C. Junior Portion | |
| 647 | 26 | 4 | 38 | Ellbro Michael | Mr J. Ellbro | West Street Childrey | — | 18 | 6 | 33 | None | 16 | 9 | 38 | Removed to Foxhill | c/o Mr Barker, Foxhill |
| 648 | 26 | 4 | 38 | Toomey Grenville | Mr Wm Toomey | West Street Childrey | — | 15 | 6 | 33 | None | 25 | 8 | 40 | To Woolton Junior School | |
| ~~[illegible]~~ 649 | 26 | 4 | 38 | Vanderwell Dawn | Mr Vanderwell | West Street Childrey | | 22 | 4 | 33 | None | 7 | 7 | 39 | Attending Marlborough Infant School pro tem. | Mother ill in Hospital |
| 651 | 9 | 5 | 38 | Palmer William James | Mr E. H. Palmer | Mill Farm E. Challow | — | 18 | 4 | 33 | None | 2 | 6 | 38 | To Sparsholt C of E | |
| 652 | 31 | 5 | 38 | Vane Frederick | Mr Albert Henry Vane | West Challow | — | 29 | 9 | 25 | Buckland | 8 | 3 | 39 | Removed to Purton | |
| 653 | 13 | 6 | 38 | Braine Herbert John Simpson | Mr Herbert J. S. Braine | The Grotto Childrey | — | 22 | 10 | 27 | Pear's Town Southampton | 27 | 3 | 39 | Collingbourne, Wilts | Address now Mill Farm, East Challow [illegible] |
| ~~[illegible]~~ 654 | " | " | " | Braine Violet Mary | " | " | — | 1 | 1 | 29 | " | 24 | 3 | 39 | Ditto | |
| 655 | " | " | " | Braine William Lewis | " | " | — | 11 | 4 | 30 | " | 27 | 3 | 39 | Ditto | |
| 656 | " | " | " | Giles Ernest Fred. Wm. | Mr G. Giles | c/o Mr G. Giles Stow Hill | — | 9 | 2 | 28 | St. Peters Devizes | 21 | 7 | 38 | Returned to home. | On holiday in Lond with Mr G Giles from last attendance to end of term |
| 657 | 20 | 6 | 38 | Vane Audrey | Mr A. H. Vane | West Challow | — | 1 | 1 | 33 | | 8 | 3 | 39 | Removed to Purton | |
| ✓ 658 | 30 | 8 | 38 | Young Francis Walter | Mr F. Young | Stow Hill | — | 12 | 9 | 33 | | 21 | 4 | 43 | To Wantage C of E Boys pro tem. | |

Admission No.	Date of Admission (or Re-Admission) Day	Mon.	Year	Full Name of Child	Name of Parent or Guardian	Address	What Exemption, if any, from Religious Instruction, is Claimed?	Date of Birth Day	Mon.	Year	Name of Last School	Date of Last Attendance at this School Day	Mon.	Year	Cause of Leaving	Remarks
✓ 659	30	8	33	Egwood May	Mr G. Egwood	Council Houses	Nil	4	9	33	None	20	7	45	To Faringdon County Girls' School.	
660	"	"	"	Pert Donald Robert	Mr R. Pert	West Challow	Nil	21	7	33		17	2	39	To Goosey C of E. pro tem. Death of Grandfather - parents gone to settle [illegible]	
✓ 661	"	"	"	Rowland Sheila Nelly	Mr C. Rowland	West St. Childrey	"	22	9	33		21	12	48	Age	
662	26	9	38	Bosley Vernon Jack	Mr Vernon Frank Bosley	Mill Farm East Challow	"	2	11	32	Grove	20	12	40	To East Challow.	
663	9	1	39	Collett Douglas Albert	Mr C. Collett	West Challow		15	11	33		31	7	40	Transferred to Wantage.	
569	9	1	39	Dance Peter Charles	Mr G. Dance	West St. Childrey	Nil	6	6	27	Hanney C of E.	31	7	41	Age.	See Pages 18 & 20.
664	23	1	39	Burnage Reginald	c/o Mrs P. Collins	Stow Hill, Childrey	Nil	2	3	31	Didcot Junior Council	3	2	39	Returned to Didcot.	X
665	"	"	"	Lynes William	Mr A.E. Lynes	Grotto Cottage	Nil	5	11	25	Upham C of E. County of Southampton	20	12	40	Age. 15	X
✓ 666	"	"	"	Lynes Edward	" "	" "	Nil	25	1	31	Ditto	21	12	44	To Findon Nr Worthing age 13	X
667	30	1	39	Burnage Dennis	c/o Mrs P. Collins	Stow Hill Childrey	Nil	18	12	32	Didcot Junior Council	3	2	39	Returned to Didcot	
668	6	3	39	Clifton Eileen May	Mr S. Clifton	West Challow	Nil	4	10	29	Coleshill	2	8	39	Gone away from district. Whereabouts not known.	
669	6	3	39	Clifton Freda Linda May	Ditto	West Challow	Nil	8	11	27	Coleshill	2	8	39		
670	7	3	39	Clifton Edwin Wm. S.	Ditto	West Challow	Nil	9	9	32	Coleshill	2	8	39	To Challow Stn. pro tem.	
660	13	3	39	Pert Donald Robert	Mr R. Pert	West Challow	Nil	21	7	33	Goosey	6	11	39	Attending Goosey School.	See Above.
671	14	3	39	Hitchens Iris	Mr W. Hitchens	West Challow	Nil	21	3	26	Bredon	17	3	39	Left District for Chieveley	
672	"	"	"	Hitchens William	" "	" "	Nil	14	7	27		"	"	"		
673	"	"	"	Hitchens Edward	" "	" "	Nil	14	1	29		"	"	"		
674	4	4	39	Badger Albert Laurence	Mr W.L. Badger	" "	Nil	8	9	26	Bampton C of E (Deanery)	13	3	40	To Shrivenham.	
675	"	"	"	Badger John Henry	"	" "	Nil	1	5	30	Aston C of E. nr Bampton	12	3	40	To Shrivenham.	
676	18	4	39	Vandervell Lorna Violet	Mr Vandervell	West St. Childrey	Nil	26	4	34	Nil.	7	7	39	Attending Marlborough Infants School Acton.	(Mother in Hospital).
677	"	"	"	Alder Jean	Mr L. Alder	East View East Challow	Nil	19	4	34	Nil	18	6	40	To East Challow School	Absent several weeks before transfer as from 18-6-40
✓ 678	"	"	"	Williams Audrey Rose	Mr W. Williams	Church St. Childrey	Nil	18	5	34	Nil	27	7	49	Age.	
679	"	"	"	Harris Brian	c/o Mrs G. Embling	West St. Childrey	Nil	5	10	33	Sunningdale	2	3	39	To Newbury	
614	18	4	39	Pottinger Linda Joy	Mr E. Pottinger	Council Houses Childrey	Nil	30	3	31	Stanford in the Vale	24	6	41	To Stanford-in-Vale pro tem.	See Pages 20 & 21.
626	"	"	"	Pottinger Ruth	Ditto	Ditto	Ditto	26	1	32	Ditto	10	5	40	To Stanford-in-Vale.	
680	22	5	39	Sykes Harold	Mr J. Sykes	West Challow	None	16	3	27	Kirtlington C of E.	9	6	39	Removed to Kingswood Aylesbury, Bucks.	Admitted Waddesdon Nr. Aylesbury, Bucks
681	"	"	"	Sykes Myrtle		" "	"	30	6	29	"	"	"	"	" "	
682	"	"	"	Sykes Marjory Winifred		"	"	12	7	29	"	"	"	"	" "	
683	6	6	39	Sykes Alan		"	"	10	12	25	"	8	6	39	Removed to Kingswood Nr. Aylesbury, Bucks.	
684	4	6	39	Sykes Rosemary		"	"				"	9	6	39	Removed to Kingswood Aylesbury, Bucks.	
642	26	6	39	Johnson Wm. James	Mr Wm. Johnson	West Challow	"	20	1	31	Nuneham C of E.	20	11	39	To Wallingford Institution	See Page 21
✓ 685	11	7	39	Simmonds Michael John Lewis	Mr R.F. Simmonds	c/o Mr G. Rowland, High St. Childrey	"	10	8	31	India	3	4	46	Left. Age.	75 Garfield Terrace Leeman Road York
686	11	9	39	Jackson Edna	c/o Mrs Williams	Church St. Childrey	"	9	5	26	Appleton Rd. Senior School York	21	3	40	Returned to York.	Canal St. Leeman Rd.
687	"	"	"	Corrie Michael	c/o Mr G. Rowland	High St. Childrey	"	4	9	29	Preston Park School Wembley	29	9	39	Returned Home.	21 Quantock [illegible] Neasden N.W.10
688	"	"	"	Welch Gwendoline Ellen	c/o Mrs R. Smith	Godfreys Farm Childrey	"	17	9	25	Mitcham Lane Council	29	9	39	Returned Home	203 [illegible] Rd. Streatham. S.W.16.
689	"	"	"	Welch Pamela Edith	"	" "	"	9	2	28	" " "	6	10	39	Returned to London	Ditto

Admission No. 23	Date of Admission (or Re-Admission) Day	Mon.	Year	Full Name of Child	Name of Parent or Guardian	Address	[illegible] Exemption, if any, [illegible] Instruction, [illegible]aimed?	Date of Birth Day	Mon.	Year	Name of Last School	Date of Last Attendance at this School Day	Mon.	Year	Cause of Leaving	Remarks
690	11	9	39	Welch Robert Reginald	c/o Mrs R. Smith	Godfreys Farm Childrey	None	28	5	33	Mitcham Lane Infants – Mitcham	13	10	39	Returned to London.	108 Hewitley Rd. Tooting
691	"	"	"	Ball Daphne Ellen	" " "	" " "	"	28	9	29	Selincourt Rd. Jun. Council Tooting	29	9	39	Returned Home	S.W.17
692	"	"	"	Taylor Douglas Charles	c/o Mrs Taylor	High St. Childrey	"	7	11	30	Marylebone Central	12	12	41	52 Marvenly House Crawford St. Mar. Rd London W.1.	52 Marvenly House Crawford St. Marylebone Rd. London W.1.
693	"	"	"	Taylor Frederick Henry	" "	" " "	"	25	12	27	Marylebone Central.	12	12	41	Returned Home to above address.	Ditto
694	"	"	"	Cox Ronald	c/o Mrs Ridley	Stow Hill "	"	[illegible]	[illegible]	[illegible]	Stroud Green Hornsey	19	1	40	Returned Home	9 Victoria Rd Stroud Green.
695	"	"	"	Cox Iris Gladys	"	" "	"	6	2	32	Stroud Green. Hornsey.	19	1	40	Returned Home.	Ditto
696	"	"	"	Crook Doreen Mary	Mr Cecil Crook	West Challow.	"	22	4	29	Stanton St. John Oxon	23	11	39	Removed to Joseliffe Hall & admitted East Challow School 27-11-39.	
697	"	"	"	Crook Christine Mary	– – –	" "	"	25	12	32	Stanton St. John Oxon.	23	11	39	Ditto above.	
698	"	"	"	Case Winifred Rose	c/o Mrs Crane	West Challow	"	12	9	29	Harwood Rd. Jun. Fulham	6	10	39	Returned Home	The 3 Stanford Place, Kings Rd Fulham.
699	"	"	"	Durrance Thomas Walter William			"	14	9	28	Avonmore Rd. West Kensington	6	10	39	" "	13 Gobnaston St. West Kensington. W.14.
700	"	"	"	Durrance Marjorie Rose	"	"	"	31	1	30	Ditto	6	10	39	" "	Ditto
701	"	"	"	Durrance William Stephen	–		"	11	3	33	Ditto.	6	10	39	" "	Ditto
702	"	"	"	Tuckey Patricia Margaret	Mr Tuckey	High St. Childrey	None	4	10	34	None.	12	3	40	To Wantage Council Pro Tem.	
632	"	"	"	Wood Robert	Mr F. Wood.	c/o Mrs R.O. Legge Post Office Childrey	None.	30	8	31	[illegible] Kent St Margarets Bay	22	9	39	To Windsor	See Page 21 & below.
638	"	"	"	Burns Jean	c/o Mrs Lewis	Chapel Cottages Childrey	None	28	2	31	North Street Council Hornchurch	27	3	45	Age.	39 Globe Way, Hornchurch Essex
703	"	"	"	Harris Sheila Theresa Eliza	c/o Mrs Hawkin	Council Houses Childrey	None	19	3	34	112 [illegible] Rd. Blackheath S.E.3.	14	12	39	Still Returned Home.	attended Sherrington Road School Charlton.
649	"	"	"	Vandervell Dawn.	Mr Vandervell	West St. Childrey	None	22	4	33	Marlborough Infants School	10	4	46	To Wollingham Pro Tem. Rose Rd Council School	
676	"	"	"	Vandervell Lorna Violet	Mr Vandervell.	" " "	None	26	4	38	Marlborough Infants School	7	4	46	to Nottingham Pro Tem. Rose Rd Council School.	
704	12	9	39	Fairburn Donald Bruce	Mr Maurice Fairburn c/o Mr Pickett West Challow	West Challow	None	27	12	32	Stroud Green for Hornsey	1	12	39	Returned to Stroud Green	13 Cromwell Rd., Stroud Green Hornsey
705	25	9	39	Wiltshire Joan Margaret	Mr E.G. Wiltshire	West St. Childrey	None	10	7	29	Risley Avenue School Tottenham.	8	11	39	To Westcott	37 Walthurst Avenue Tottenham N17
706	"	"	"	Wiltshire Allan Peter	Do.	Do.	Do.	19	2	34	Ditto	8	11	39	To Westcott.	Ditto
523	"	"	"	Mepstead Jean Evelyn	Mrs W. Mepstead	c/o Mr Hammond West [illegible]	None.	31	3	26	Rochester	12	12	39	Returned to Rochester.	61 Morden St. Rochester, Kent.
651	31	10	39	Palmer William James	Mr E.H. Palmer	College Farm Cottages	None	18	4	33	Sparsholt C of E.	29	1	45	Age.	
707	"	"	"	Palmer Jean	Mr E. H. Palmer	College Farm Cottages	None	16	2	27	Sparsholt C of E	13	1	41	Absent with infection for [illegible]	
660	20	11	39	Pert Donald Robert	Mr R Pert	West Challow	None	21	7	33	Goosey	9	1	40	To Goosey School [illegible]	
632	27	11	39	Wood Robert	Mr F. Wood	c/o Mrs R.O. Legge Post Office Childrey	None	30	8	31	St Margarets Bay, Kent.	6	12	39	Returned to St. Margarets Bay	See Above & Page 21.
708	3	1	40	Rowland Mervyn.	Mr S. Rowland	C. Houses Childrey	None	9	10	34	None	27	7	49	Transferred to Wantage C. School Senior Group.	
709	"	"	"	Stratton Dorothy Ann.	Mr R. Stratton	West Challow	None.	8	12	34		3	5	46	Northfield Farm. To Long Wittenham.	
710	12	3	40	Hill Charles.	c/o Mrs Greener c/o Mr W. Panting	Council Houses Childrey	None	4	4	28	St. Matthias. Poplar.	21	3	40	Returned to London	60 Chiltern St. Poplar. (with married sister)
711	"	"	"	Hill Edward Daniel	"			7	3	31	St. Matthias Poplar.	21	3	40	Returned to London	
712	2	4	40	Green David Joseph	Mr J. Green	Council Houses W Chal[low]	"	7	3	35		27	7	49	Transferred to Wantage Council Senior Group.	
632	2	4	40	Wood Robert	Mr F. Wood	c/o Mr R.O. Legge Post Office Childrey	"	30	8	31	St. Margarets Bay Kent.	19	4	40	Returned to St Margarets Bay.	
660	22	4	40	Pert Donald Robert	Mr R Pert	West Challow	"	21	7	33	Goosey	2	4	43	To Goosey pro tem	(See above & Previous pages.
713	14	5	40	Walsh Patricia Margaret	Mr T. Walsh	c/o Mrs King Childrey Manor House, Mr S[illegible]	Roman Catholic	11	1	30	Richmond R.C. Richmond Yorks	14	7	41	To Faringdon County Girls	
714	14	5	40	Walsh Michael Leo	"	"		7	2	35	Barton C of E Nr Richmond Yorks	30	7	46	Scholarship to King Alfred School, Wantage.	Removed to The Stables, Stoneleigh Abbey, Kenilworth, Warwick.
626	20	5	40	Pottinger Ethel [illegible]	Mr E. Pottinger	Council Houses Chal[low]	None	28	6	32	Stanford-in-Vale	24	6	41	Stanford-in-Vale Pro tem	See Page 20. 21 [illegible]
715	20	5	40	Soa[illegible] Eleanor Mary	c/o Mr J. [illegible]	Stow Hill Childrey	None	8	5	31	Crescent Rd. Erith	25	7	40	Returned to Erith	

24

Admission No.	Date of Admission (or Re-Admission) Day	Mon	Year	Full Name of Child	Name of Parent or Guardian	Address	What Exemption, if any, from Religious Instruction is Claimed?	Date of Birth Day	Mon	Year	Name of Last School he attended before entering this School. If this is his first School the word "None" must be entered.	Date of Last Attendance at this School Day	Mon	Year	Cause of Leaving	Remarks (Private Addresses)
716	5	6	40	Spanton Barbara Irene	Mrs. Irene Spanton	c/o Mrs J. Jurls. Snr. Stow Hill Childrey	None	26	8	31	Westborough Rd. C. School Westcliff - Southend.	6	3	43	Returned to Southend.	E. (Private) 5 Macdonald Avenue Westcliff Southend
717	24	6	40	Spanton Peter	c/o Mrs J. Jurls.	Mount Pleasant Stow Hill	None	1	1	33	Ashdown Private School Lee, Southend (Evacuated) Privately	18	10	40	Returned to Westcliffe-on-Sea (Supposed to be returning). Kept on Register.	Inverois School, Bostall Lane, Abbey Wood. E. (Private)
718	"	"	"	Hardman John Henry	Mr Vandervell.	Mr Vandervell West St.	None	10	11	29	Melbourn, Cambs. (A Private Coach - See Note.	10	10	40	Left District.	E (Private) 33 Manor Rd. Abbey Wood Woolwich S.E.2.
703	24	6	40	Harris Sheila Theresa	c/o Mrs Hawkins	No. 7 Council Houses Childrey	None	17	3	34	Kidbrook Park School Blackheath S.E.3.	22	3	43	Returned Home pro tem.	E. (Private) 112 [illegible] Rd. Blackheath
719	17	6	40	Horn Jean Margaret	Mrs G. Pottinger	West St. Childrey	None	19	5	26	Goresbrook Snr. Girls Dagenham	15	8	40	Returned to Dagenham 17.8.40	E 45 Cartwright Rd. Dagenham.
720	"	"	"	Calvert Eva Joyce	Mrs Morse	May's Farm West Challow.	None	2	7	26	Goresbrook Snr. Girls	15	8	40	Returned to Dagenham.	E 45 Chaplin Road Dagenham.
721	"	"	"	Hostler Florence	Mr Collett.	Coppice Leaze Farm W. Challow	"	10	4	26	" "	15	8	40	Returned to Dagenham 17.8.40	E 29 Chaplin Rd. Dagenham
722	"	"	"	Hostler Ivy	Mr Collett.	Coppice Leaze Farm W. Challow	None	10	4	26.	" "	25	6	40	Returned to Dagenham. On Register until 19.7.40 Excluded for Measles.	E Ditto.
723	"	"	"	Calvert Ethel Joan	Mrs Morse	May's Farm, West Challow	None.	2	6	28.	" "	15	8	40	Returned to Dagenham.	E See 720.
724	"	"	"	Hostler Iris	Mr Collett	Coppice Leaze Farm W. Challow.	None	22	4	28	"	15	6	40	Returned to Dagenham 17.8.40.	E See 721.
725	"	"	"	McDonald William James	Mr J. Breakspear.	3 Council Houses, Childrey	None	2	10	27	Goresbrook Snr. Boys	3	7	40.	Returned to Dagenham. Actually on, Excluded for Measles.	E 39 Kullington Rd. Dagenham
726	"	"	"	Potter John	Mr C. Young	Cornhill Farm W. Challow.	None	26	9	27	" " "	14	9	41	Returned to Dagenham.	E 23 Sinnington Rd. Dagenham.
727	"	"	"	Dowers Frederick Thomas	Mrs E. Froud.	Pond Farm Childrey	None	20	1	27	" " "	24	10	41	To Employment ~~[illegible]~~ Left Age.	E 99 Tilney Rd. Dagenham
728	"	"	"	Heaviside Edward	Mrs E. Froud	Pond Farm	None	25	7	27	" " "	16	12	41	Returned to Dagenham.	E 117 Hedgemans Rd. Dagenham
729	"	"	"	Couchman Ronald Albert.	Mrs P. Prendergast.	6 Council Houses Childrey	None	22	2	27	" " "	17	1	41	Returned to Dagenham 19.1.41.	E 82 Cartwright Rd. Dagenham.
730	"	"	"	Elder George Robert.	Mr A. Winterbourne	9 Council Houses Childrey	None	6	2	27	" " "	18	7	41	Returned to Dagenham	E 29 Hatfield Rd. Dagenham.
731	"	"	"	Shorter Robert Edward.	Mr R. Pert.	Fernlea. West Challow	None.	8	9	27	" " "	14	8	41	Returned to Dagenham.	E 47 Cartwright Rd. Dagenham.
732	"	"	"	Horn Peter William	Mrs G. Rowland.	Lester House, High St. Childrey	None	21	9	27	" " "	12	2	41	Returned to Dagenham	E See 719.
733	"	"	"	Shorter David Leslie	Mr R. Pert	Fernlea. West Challow	None	30	8	29	Dagenham Finneymore Rd. Junior	14	8	41	Returned to Dagenham	E See 731.
734	"	"	"	Short Caroline Eliz.	Mrs P. Collins	Stow Hill, Childrey	None	1	1	29	– – –	2	10	40	2/10/40 Returned to Dagenham	E 4 Waltham Gardens Dagenham
735	"	"	"	Fish Lillian Ruth	Mrs G. Capwood.	10 Council Offices Childrey	None	15	11	29	" – –	27	6	41	To The Laurels, Moss Lane Alderley Edge - Shropshire.	E 4 Cartwright Rd. Dagenham.
736	"	"	"	Fish Ruth Emma	Mrs Palmer	The Grotto, Childrey	None	5	11	30	– " –	27	6	41	Ditto.	E See 735.
737	"	"	"	Griffiths Joan	Mrs E. Bedford	The Grotto, Childrey	None	7	12	30	– " "	19	12	41	Returned to Ilford	E 43 Coleman Rd. Dagenham [illegible]
738	"	"	"	Johnson Rose Beatrice Mary	Mrs A. Pettifer	Stow Hill, Childrey	None	6	10	30	" " –	5	11	40	To "Oaklands" Clinic Wokingham 21.11.40.	E 75 Farm St. Devon Rd. Barking
739	"	"	"	Short Irene Joyce	Mrs A. Pettifer	Stow Hill, Childrey	None	13	8	30	" – –	4	7	41	Returned Home to Dagenham.	E See 734.
740	"	"	"	Potter Eileen Joyce	Mrs H. Legge.	Cornhill Farm West Challow	None				– " "	15	5	42	Returned to Dagenham	E See 726
741	"	"	"	Calvert Iris Winifred	Mrs Morse	May's Farm, West Challow.	None				– " –	15	8	40	Returned to Dagenham.	E See 720.
742	"	"	"	Dowers Sylvia Joan	Mr E. Bell.	West St. Childrey	None	11	5	31	" " "	23	12	42	To Sparsholt.	~~E~~ See 727. Now a resident
743	"	"	"	Simmons Rose	Mrs G. Jenner c/o Mrs F. Ellis	High St. Childrey West St. Childrey	None	18	12	31	– " "	14	5	41	Returned to Dagenham.	E 33 Coleman Rd. Dagenham. See also Page 6
744	"	"	"	Lawson Joyce	Mrs E. Pottinger c/o Prendergast	~~4 Council Houses, Childrey~~ 8 Council Houses Childrey	None	6	4	32	" " "	18	3	42	Returned to Dagenham	E 50 Coleman Rd. Dagenham
745	"	"	"	Elder Ronald	Mr A. Winterbourne	9 Council Houses, Childrey	None	7	5	27	– – –	27	3	41	In Hospital from 3.4.41 till returning to Dagenham. Parent refusing treatment.	E See 730. See date of return of brother
746	"	"	"	Potter George Alfred	Mr C. Young	Cornhill Farm. West Challow	None	20	3	~~34~~ 29	" " "	15	5	42	To Dagenham for holiday - Did not return	E See 726
747	"	"	"	Simmons William John	Mr R. Rea	Dropshort, Childrey	None	5	9	30	" " "	26	9	41	Returned to Dagenham	E See 743 See also Page 6.
748	"	"	"	Lawson Eric	Mr J. Shealler	2 Council ~~Offices~~ Houses Childrey	None	16	7	33	" " "	13	3	42	Returned to Dagenham	E See 744.
749	"	"	"	Fish Leonard	Mrs Palmer	The Grotto, Childrey	None	31	12	33	" " "	27	6	41	To - The Laurels, Moss Lane Alderley Edge, Shropshire	E See 7[illegible]

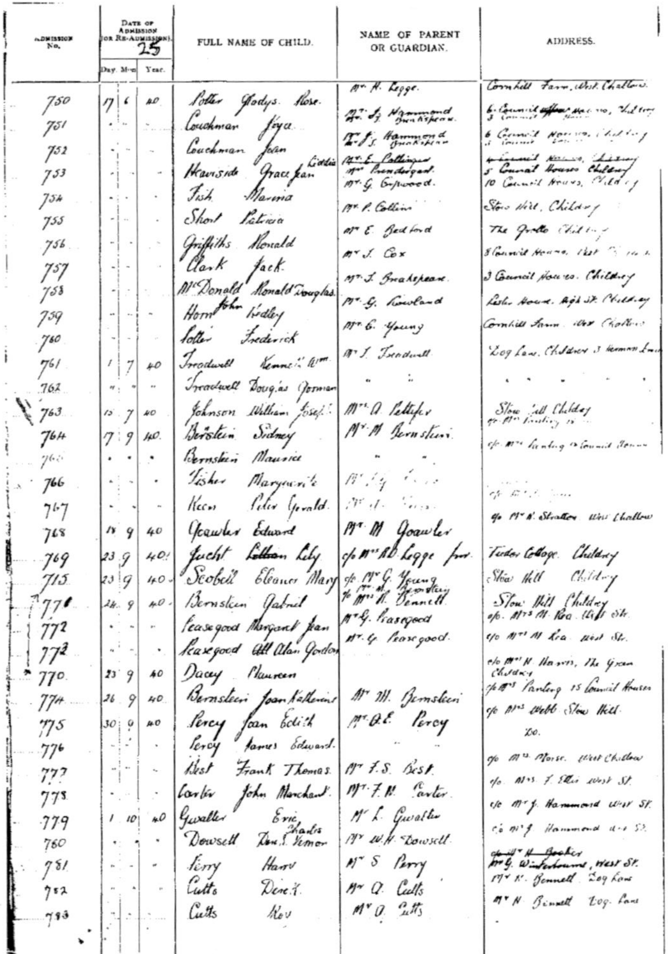

ADMISSION No.	DATE OF ADMISSION (OR RE-ADMISSION) 25 Day	Month	Year	FULL NAME OF CHILD.	NAME OF PARENT OR GUARDIAN.	ADDRESS.
750	17	6	40	Potter Gladys Rose	Mr H. Legge	Cornhill Farm, West Challow
751				Couchman Joyce	Mr J. Hammond / Mr J. Breakspear	6 Council Houses, Childrey / 3 Council Houses
752				Couchman Jean	Mr J. Hammond / Mr J. Breakspear	6 Council Houses, Childrey / 3 Council Houses
753				Hawside Grace Jean Liddie	~~Mr E. Collinge~~ Mrs Prendergast	~~4 Council Houses, Childrey~~ 5 Council Houses Childrey
754				Fish Marina	Mr G. Gopwood.	10 Council Houses, Childrey
755				Short Patricia	Mr P. Collins	Stow Hill, Childrey
756				Griffiths Ronald	Mr E. Bedford	The Grotto Childrey
757				Clark Jack	Mr J. Cox	8 Council Houses, West [illegible]
758				McDonald Ronald Douglas	Mr J. Breakspear	3 Council Houses. Childrey
759				Horn John Ridley	Mr G. Rowland	Leslie House, High St. Childrey
760				Potter Frederick	Mr E. Young	Cornhill Farm West Challow
761	1	7	40	Treadwell Kenneth Wm	Mr J. Treadwell	Dog Lane, Childrey 3 Herman Lane
762	"	"	"	Treadwell Douglas Norman	" "	" " "
763	15	7	40	Johnson William Joseph	Mrs A. Pettifer	Stow Hill Childrey / c/o Mrs Pauling 15
764	17	9	40	Bernstein Sidney	Mr M Bernstein	c/o Mrs Pauling 15 Council Houses
765				Bernstein Maurice	" "	
766				Fisher Marguerite	[illegible]	[illegible]
767				Keen Peter Gerald	[illegible]	c/o Mr R. Stratton West Challow
768	18	9	40	Goawler Edward	Mr M Goawler	
769	23	9	40	Jucht ~~Lillian~~ Lily	c/o Mrs A.D. Legge for	Tudor Cottage Childrey
715	23	9	40	Scobell Eleanor Mary	c/o Mr G. Young	Stow Hill Childrey
771	24	9	40	Bernstein Gabriel	c/o Mrs M. Bernstein / c/o Mrs H. Dennett	Stow Hill Childrey
772				Peasegood Margaret Jean	Mr G. Peasegood	c/o Mrs M. Rea West St.
773				Peasegood Alan Gordon	Mr G. Peasegood.	c/o Mrs M Rea West St.
770	23	9	40	Dacey Maureen		c/o Mrs N. Harris, The Green Childrey
774	26	9	40	Bernstein Joan Katherine	Mr M. Bernstein	c/o Mrs Pauling 15 Council Houses
775	30	9	40	Percy Joan Edith	Mr A.E. Percy	c/o Mrs Webb Stow Hill.
776				Percy James Edward.		Do.
777				Best Frank Thomas.	Mr F.S. Best.	c/o Mrs Morse. West Challow
778				Carter John Marchant.	Mr F.N. Carter.	c/o Mrs F. Ellis West St.
779	1	10	40	Gwalter Eric	Mr L. Gwalter	c/o Mr J. Hammond West St.
780				Dowsett Dennis Charles Vernon	Mr W.H. Dowsett.	c/o Mr J. Hammond West St.
781				Perry Harry	Mr S Perry	~~c/o Mrs H. Booker~~ Mrs G. Winterbourne, West St.
782				Cutts Derek	Mr A. Cutts	Mr H. Bennett Dog Lane
783				Cutts Rex	Mr A. Cutts	Mr H. Bennett Dog Lane

Unfortunately this section of the register has been lost.

Admission No.	Date of Admission (or Re-Admission) 26 Day	Mon	Year	Full Name of Child	Name of Parent or Guardian	Address	What Exemption, if any, from Religious Instruction is Claimed?	Date of Birth Day	Mon	Year	Name of Last School he attended before entering this School. If this is his first School the word "None" must be entered.	Date of Last Attendance at this School Day	Mon	Year	Cause of Leaving	Remarks 26
																Private Addresses
784	1	10	40	Haven Joan	Mrs C. Cowley	c/o Mrs C. Cowley High St Childrey	None	26	1	33	City Council, Canterbury	25	7	41	Taken home by parent 26.7.41. E	30 Hamsfield Rd. Walthamstow E.17. Chase Rd. [illegible] South Woodford E18. 6 Olive St. Canterbury
785	2	10	40	Saffery Lillian Helen	Mrs A. Saffery	c/o Mrs [illegible] Upper Farm W. Challow	None	17	6	27	Sparsholt C/E. Fernymoulds [illegible]	12	3	41	Returned to Canterbury E	43 Hatfield Rd. Dagenham
786	7	10	40	Tilley Ivy Elizabeth	Mr W. C. Tilley	c/o Mrs P. Bussey. Dog Lane Childrey	"	12	8	29	Ditto	30	5	41	Removed to Sparsholt E	Do. above
787	7	10	40	Tilley Ethel Mary	" "	c/o Mrs P. Bussey. Dog Lane Childrey	"	5	4	31	[illegible] Rd. Dagenham	30	5	41	Removed to Sparsholt E	
763	7	10	40	Johnson Wm. Joseph	Mrs A. Pettifer	c/o Mrs A. Pettifer Stow Hill Childrey	"	5	2	34	Deansbrook C. School Mill Hill Edgware	5	11	40	To "Oaklands" clinic Wokingham 21.10.40. Awaiting [illegible] E	See 7.56
788	18	10	40	Ludwig Joanna		c/o Mr G. Froud. College Farm Childrey	"	22	9	30		30	5	41	Returned to Mill Hill P.E	16 Lovelly Gardens N.W.7 Mill Hill
789	29	10	40	Pike Tony Victor	Mr A. Pike c/o Mr J. Green	No 7 Council Houses West Challow	"	2	11	28	Walsgrave Colliery Council School Coventry	23	12	42	Age. P.E	6 Miles Meadows Bell Green, Coventry
790	4	11	40	Taylor Shelagh	Mrs A. L. Taylor	c/o Mrs Lauder, The Close	"	11	5	33	The Gonville School Gonville Rd. Thornton Heath	9	6	42	Returned to Croydon P.E	33 Ringwood Avenue West Croydon. [illegible]
791	18	11	40	Ascott June	Mr Edwin Fredk. Ascott	c/o Mrs Hatherall. – West Challow	"	13	4	29	Grange Hill Central Sch Edgeware	30	4	41	Returned Home 14.5.41 but of School [illegible] P.E	139 Watling Avenue Burnt Oak Edgeware
792	"	"	"	Ascott Joan	" " "	" "	"	13	4	29	Ditto	13	5	41	Returned Home 14.5.41 P.E	Ditto
793	19	11	40	Aldridge Belle Matilda	Mr J. W. Aldridge	Hatchet Lane Childrey	"	31	12	27	Culvert Council School Tottenham N.15	19	12	41	Age. P.E	12 Suffolk Rd. Tottenham N.15
794	2	12	40	West Roy Alfred	Mrs O. West	c/o Mrs Morse, Mays Farm West Challow	"	21	2	34	Woodlands Rd. School Ilford	11	12	40	Returned to Ilford P.E	108 Eton Rd. Ilford
795	10	12	40	German Pearl Grace	Mr W. F. German	c/o Mr J. Beckett West Challow	"	22	1	33	Sefton Rd. School Sholing Southampton	20	12	40	Returned home P.E	15 Bellon Rd. Bulls Rd. Sholing Southampton
796	"	"	"	German Kenneth Raymond	" "	" "	"	5	10	34	Middle Rd. Infants Sholing Southampton	20	12	40	Returned home P.E	
797	6	1	41	Brown Patricia Ann	Mr W. P. Brown	Fair View, West Challow	"	6	1	36	None	10	8	42	Returned home [illegible] P.E	33 Lemmon Avenue Benton Newcastle-on-Tyne
798	"	"	"	Harris Eileen Mary	R.P.F.	c/o Mr Hawton C. Hoare	"	31	12	35	None	22	3	43	Returned home for [illegible] P.E	Wrekinmouth Rd. Blackheath
799	"	"	"	Waddle Evelyn Marie	Mr H. Waddle	c/o The Manor Childrey	"	12	6	30	Haberdashers' Askes	24	4	42	To Oxford High School for Girls P.E	53 Princes Gardens West Acton
800	"	"	"	Waddle Alison Jean	R.P.E. "	" "	"	31	5	33	"	28	4	42	To Oxford High School for Girls P.E	"
801	24	2	41	Waller Irene Janet	c/o	c/o Mrs G. Giles, The Crown Childrey	"	19	5	33	St. Peters' Devizes	25	4	41	Left District	
802	"	"	"	Paradise Betty Louisa Frances		" " "	"	9	4	27	St. Peters' Devizes	10	3	41	Returned to Devizes	
803	7	4	41	Davis Edward Roy	c/o Mr S. J. Davis	FretHorn Cottage Childrey	"	11	3	28	Wallingford Council	13	8	41	Left District To Abingdon? E	21 Lottie St. Bermondsey S.E.16
804	22	4	41	Reed James Henry	c/o Mr G. Rowland	High St. Childrey	"	8	5	31	East Lane Bermondsey	[illegible]	12	42	Returned home E	21 Lottie St. Bermondsey S.E.
805	"	"	"	Reed Michael Patrick	"	" "	"	11	11	33	" " "	"	"	"	" " E	156 Rodney Place, New Kent Rd. S.E.17 / 76 [illegible] Rd. New Kent Rd. Buildings
806	"	"	"	Dunn Eileen Josephine	Mr O. Froud, The Hatchet	The Hatchet, Childrey	"	18	4	31	Victory Place – Bermondsey	5	4	42	Returned Home E	21 Silvester St. S.E.1. St. Davis St.
807	"	"	"	Robinson Frederick Thomas	c/o Mr G. Whitehorne	West St. Childrey	"	4	4	33	Lollard St. (Southwark)	19	12	41	Returned Home E	102 [illegible] Buildings [illegible] St. 26 Valnay St. S.W.17 (Tooting)
808	"	"	"	Hill Kathleen	c/o Mr E. Pottinger	No. 4 Council Houses Childrey	"	13	3	34	Undine St. Tooting	17	10	41	To Denchworth E	64 Warlock Rd. Paddington W.9
809	"	"	"	Pocock Christine May	c/o Mr G. Cripwood	Council Houses, Childrey	"	27	7	35	Warrington Rd. Paddington	17	10	41	Returned Home E	64 Warlock Rd. Paddington W.9
810	"	"	"	Pocock Doreen Ann	" "	" "	"	11	9	33	" "	17	10	41	E	40 Yelverton Rd. S.W.11
811	"	"	"	Ralph Eileen	Morse Mrs Mays Farm	Mays Farm West Challow, Wantage	"	23	2	32	St. Mary's	17	11	41	Returned Home E	40 Yelverton Rd. S.W.11
812	"	"	"	Ralph George	c/o Mr R. Stratton	West Challow	"	17	11	33	St. Mary's	17	11	41	" E	12 Hepworth Rd. S.W.16
813	"	"	"	Stacey Barbara	c/o Mrs Morse	May's Farm, West Challow	"	10	12	32	High Path, Colliers' Wood	7	11	41	" E	12 Hepworth Rd. S.W.16
814	"	"	"	Stacey John Leslie	c/o Mr R. Stratton	West Challow	"	7	1	34	High Path, Colliers' Wood	7	11	41	"	1 Stanfield Rd. W.12
815	"	"	"	Harrison John Frederick	c/o Mr R. Stratton	West Challow	"	23	4	34	Hounslow?	28	9	43	Returned to 7 The Lawns, Hounslow. Bath Rd. Middlesex	56 Bath Rd. Hounslow. 26 Worlingham Rd. S.E.22
816	"	"	"	Webster Maurice David	c/o Mrs Lester	~~26 Worlingham Rd. East Dulwich~~ S.E.22	"	28	6	35	St. Michael's St. John Dulwich	31	7	42	Returned Home for leave & did not return again	No. 46 [illegible] Rd.
817	"	"	"	Pottinger Raymond	c/o Mr G. Pottinger	West St. Childrey	"	24	7	32	C. School, Wantage	2	4	42	Returned to Parents	Chiglemoor [illegible] Grendwell

Admission No. 27	Date of Admission (or Re-Admission) Day	Mon	Year	Full Name of Child.	Name of Parent or Guardian.	Address.	What Exemption, if any, from Religious Instruction is Claimed?	Date of Birth Day	Mon	Year	Name of Last School he attended before entering this School. If this is his first School the word "None" must be entered.	Date of Last Attendance at this School Day	Mon	Year	Cause of Leaving.	Remarks. 27
818	23	4	41	Pritchard Elizabeth	c/o Mrs Cocks	4 Council Houses W. Challow	None	6	12	35	Oxford Gardens.	7	5	41	Removed to Kennel Gate Clinic 12-6-41 during absence under medical advice E.	36 Peabody Estate, Dalgarno Gardens North Kensington. London W.10.
✓ 819	"	"	"	Salt Pamela	Mrs Salt	c/o Mrs A.V. Law, High St. Childrey	"	13	11	30	Grove Lane, Wantage. Hamstel Lane Southend	23	7	43	Returned to Southend P.E. 71 [illegible] St. Southend-on-Sea	37 Lovelace Gardens Southend.
820	28	4	41	Clark Barbara Irene	Mr Charles Ed. Clark	White Cottage, Childrey	"	22	4	36	NONE	11	7	41	Returned to previous address in Hayes. Middx.	45 Yeading Gardens, Hayes Middlesex.
821	19	5	41	Dance Edna	Mr C. Dance	Council Houses West St. Childrey	"	10	1	36	None.	19	9	41	Left District	100 Crown St. Lowestoft.
✓ 822	11	6	41	Collins John Albert	Mr P. Collins	Stow Hill Childrey	"	27	6	36	None	29	7	48	To Wantage C.	
650	11	6	41	Collins Dorothy	Mr P. Collins	Stow Hill Childrey.	"	27	4	33	Didcot Council Junior	9	10	42	To Didcot pro tem	See other Admission Register.
763	23	6	41	Johnson Wm. Joseph	c/o Mrs Johnson, Childrey / c/o Mrs Busy, Dog Lane	Dog Lane "	"	5	2	34	Re-admitted from Clinic	2	7	41	Removed to Clinic [illegible] Wantage. Left District	See Pages 2 & 3. 246 Whitehorse Rd. S. Norwood
✓ 823	14	7	41	Brook Shirley	Mr Ed. Brook	c/o Mrs Marsden. W. Challow.	"	26	12	34	Wroughton Wilts	26	2	43	P.E	taken away suddenly by father. Domestic trouble. (no address left or sent)
614	14	7	41	Pottinger Linda Joy	Mr E. Pottinger	4 Council Houses Childrey	"	30	3	31	Stanford-in-Vale.	29	3	45	Age. - To Employment.	} See Previous Admission Register.
626	"	"	"	Pottinger Ruth	" "	" "	"	26	6	32	" " "	30	7	46.	Age - To Employment	}
743	28	7	41	Simmons Rose	c/o Mrs A. Pettifer / Mrs Cornish	Stow Hill Childrey	"	18	12	31	Fanshawe Rd. Junior Dagenham.	26	9	41	Returned to Dagenham	2nd Evacuation from Dagenham to Childrey. See Page 1
824	1	8	41	Fisher Julia Ann.	Mrs J. Hammond	No 6 Council Houses, Childrey	"	~~14~~	~~8~~	~~41~~	None	14	8	41	Returned Home. P.E	15 Concanon Road Brixton S.W.2.
825	"	"	"	Simmons Mary	c/o Mrs D. Pettifer	Stow Hill	"	21	10	36.	None.	26	9	41	Returned to Dagenham E.	53. Coleman Rd. Dagenham.
✓ 826	16	9	41	Simpson Stanley	Mr Simpson.	The Green, Childrey	"	14	1	30	Faringdon Senior	6	4	44	Age. - To Employment	
✓ 827	"	"	"	Simpson Elsie Lily	"	" " "	"	15	11	34	Stanford-in-Vale.	29	7	49	To Wantage C.	
✓ 828	"	"	"	Lines Alan John Richard	Mr Lines	c/o Mr Smith, Coffin [illegible] W. Challow	"	20	11	32.	Goosey.	10	8	44	To King Alfred's School Wantage. P.E.	23 Boileau Rd. Barnes S.W.13 {[illegible] Rd School}
[illegible]	"	"	"	Williams Ronald Wm.	Mr W. Williams.	Church St. Childrey		29	7	34	None	29	7	49	To Wantage C.	
[illegible]	22	9	41	Edgar Geoffrey David	Mrs Edgar	c/o Mr [illegible] Farm, The Old Manor Childrey	"	5	4	32	Harrow Weald [illegible]	19	3	43	Removed to [illegible] Kintbury	Attending Kintbury St. Mary's
✓ 831	4	11	41	McGregor Graham John	Mr McGregor	c/o Mr W. Turner, Council Houses Childrey	"	21	10	34	Sparsholt C of E.	5	7	46	To Arundel.	Now West Ewell. Nr. Epsom.
✓ 832	17	11	41	Brown Denis John	Mr F. Brown	Petwick Farm, Childrey	"	11	5	30	Goosey	10	2	43.	To Stockcross School pro tem.	Benham Park [illegible] Marsh Benham Newbury, Berks. See Page 5.
581	5	1	42	Haines Brian	Mr F.J. Haines	Council Houses. W. Challow	"	28	6	29	Gt. Coxwell C of E	30	7	43	Age. - To Employment	
✓ 833	"	"	"	Bungay Margaret Ann	Mr W. Bungay	Council Houses Childrey	"	19	2	37	None.	20	7	50	Transferred to Wantage County at 13.	
✓ 834	"	"	"	Pert Bryan Henry Mervyn	Mr R. Pert.	West Challow	"	4	1	37	None.	2	4	43	To Goosey pro tem.	
835	"	"	"	Hammond Rose Joyce Mary	Mr J. Hammond	West Challow.	"	26	7	24	East Challow C of E.	6	2	42	To Luckington Wilts.	See below.
836	12	1	42	Hammond Trevor Bryan		" "	"	8	1	28.	East Challow "	2	4	42	Age. To Employment.	
837	16	3	43	Wooldridge Edward Cecil	Mr Wooldridge	West Challow	"	14	7	34	Crookham Nr. Newbury.	2	4	42	Left District To Bordon, Hants	
838	"	"	"	Wooldridge Pamela Rose	"	" "	"	5	6	32	" "	2	4	42	Left District	
839	"	"	"	Wooldridge Maisie Evelyn	"	" "	"	7	10	35	" "	-	-	-	"	
✓ 747	13	4	42	Simmons William	c/o Mrs E. Cornish	Stow Hill, Childrey	"	5	9	30	Goresbrook Senior Dagenham	21	5	43	Returned to Dagenham.	{See also Page 1. Not an evacuee on return.}
✓ 840	14	4	42.	Harrison Thomas Derrick	c/o Miss Stallen	West Challow	"	16	2	37	Transferred from Aldburgh [illegible] Nr Harleston, Norfolk	28	9	45	Returned to 7 The Lawns, [illegible] Rd Hounslow. Middlesex. E	Home address [illegible] Rd. Hounslow. Middlesex
✓ 841	"	"	"	Read James Robert	Mrs Read.	c/o Miss Abs. Stow Hill	"	13	2	37	None.	20	7	50	Transferred to Wantage County @ 13. E.	39 Findhorn St. Poplar E.14.
835	1	6	42	Hammond Rose Joyce	Mr J. Hammond	West Challow	"	21	7	34	Luckington Wilts	30	7	42	Left district to stay with a relative.	See above
✓ 842	13	7	42	Bosley Claude	Mr Bosley	East Challow	"	10	6	35	Wantage C of E.	29	7	48	To Wantage County School.	
✓ 843				Mason Winnifred Mary	Mr J. Mason	Greendown Farm.	"	13	9	30	Letcombe Bassett	31/15	11	44	Age.	
✓ 844	4	8	42	Breakspear Sheila	Mr J. Breakspear	3 Council Houses Childrey	"	6	9	37.	None	4	7	51	To Wantage County School	

Admission No.	Date of Admission (or Re-Admission) 28 Day	Mon	Year	Full Name of Child.	Name of Parent or Guardian.	Address.	What Exemption, if any, from Religious Instruction is Claimed?	Date of Birth. Day	Mon	Year	Name of Last School he attended before entering this School. If this is his first School the word "None" must be entered.	Date of Last Attendance at this School. Day	Mon	Year	Cause of Leaving.	Remarks. 28
✓ 845	4	8	42	Vandervell Hubert Daniel	Mr Vandervell.	5 Council Houses Childrey	None	11	11	37	None	20	4	48	To Lascoe Rd. Council Hanger. Notts.	Left Term - On Holiday.
✓ 846	4	8	42	McGregor Anthony Wm.	Mr McGregor	" " "	None				None.	20	7	50	Transferred to Wantage County School at 13.	
847	15	9	42	Buckland Robert Nigel " " Keith	Mr Buckland	Dog Lane, Childrey	None	13	1	37	North Cerney Cirencester	23	10	42	[illegible] Farm To Highworth [illegible]	135 Waye Avenue, Cranford Hounslow. Middx
✓ 848	"	"	"	Chand Griffiths	c/o Mrs Stratton, West Challow.	Bridge Farm W. Challow	None	30	10	32	Cranford - Hounslow	20	7	45	Returned Home.	
✓ 849	3	11	42	Iles Dorothy Jean	Mr Charles R. Iles	Dog Lane, Childrey	None	14	8	33	Coleshill C of E	27	1	43	To Hannington Nr Highworth	
850	"	"	"	Iles Cyril Frederick James	" "	" "	"	15	11	34	" "	"	"	"	Do.	See Also at Page 7. See also [illegible]
✓ 650	3	11	42	Collins Dorothy	Mr P. Collins	Stow Hill	"	27	4	33	Didcot Junior		7	48	Age.	See Previous Pages entry
851	6	1	43	Cullis Peter Thomas	Major [illegible]	East Manton Stalls	None	17	9	30	[illegible] Common, Coventry	18	12	44	Age.	
852	"	"	"	Breakspear Frederick Stuart	c/o Mrs G. Winterbourne	West St. Childrey	None	20	2	33	Upper Basildon. Berks	2	2	43	Returned to Basildon	
853	"	"	"	Breakspear Raymond John	" "	" "	"	"	"	"	" " "	2	2	43	Returned to Basildon	
854	"	"	"	Breakspear Pearl Louise	" "	" "	"	[illegible]	6	35	" " "	"	"	"	Do	
855	"	"	"	Williams Raymond Edward	Mr W. Williams	Daisy Cottage "	"	25	1	38	[illegible]	22	9	50	To Linton Lane Boys' Modern School Epsom.	
~~8~~ 835	"	"	"	Hammond Rosey Joyce Mary	Mr J. Hammond	West Challow	"	26	7	34	Junior School	8	1	43	To Luckington Wilts	Address Pendennis Park, Bristol (Two Entries Page 4)
[illegible]	7	1	43	Cox Kay [illegible]	Mr T. Cox	West Challow	"	7	12	37	[illegible]	24	7	51	To Wantage County School.	
832	12	4	43	Brown Denis John	Mrs F. Brown	Petwick Farm.	"	11	5	30	Stockcross (See Page 4).				Left to Employment.	See Also Page 4
703	19	4	43	Harris Sheila Thirza	c/o Mrs Hawtin	No 7 Council Houses Childrey	"	19	3	34	Did not attend School during stay in London.	16	7	43	Returned Home for Temp. Holidays & did not return	See Previous Register
798	"	"	"	Harris Eileen Mary	" "	" " " "	"	31	12	35	Do.	"	"	"	Ditto	" " "
835	4	5	43	Hammond Rose Joyce Mary	Mr J. Hammond	West Challow	"	26	7	34		10	8	44	To Horton Hillside Horton, Gloucestershire	See Also Page 4.
660	"	"	"	Pert Donald Robert	Mrs R. Pert	West Challow	"	21	7	33	Goosey C of E	30	7	48	Left age.	See Previous Register.
834	"	"	"	Pert Bryan Mervyn Henry	" "	" "	"	4	1	37	Goosey C of E	20	7	50	Transferred to Wantage County at 13	See also Page 4.
857	4	5	43	Palmer Roger	Mr E.H. Palmer	The Grotto Childrey	"	7	5	38	None	24	7	51	To Wantage County School	
858	"	"	"	Bosley Maurice Kenneth	Mr F.V. Bosley	Mill Farm East Challow	"	24	1	38	"	24	7	51	To Wantage County School	
859	"	"	"	Brown Peter William	Mr W. Brown	West Challow	"	7	5	38	"	24	7	51	To Wantage County B School	
860	31	5	43	Hammond Richard John	Mr J. Hammond	West Challow	"	25	4	38	"	10	8	44	To Horton Hillside Horton, Gloucestershire	
861	7	6	43	Sayer Brian	Mr Norman Sayer	c/o Mrs Saunders The Close Childrey	"	16	7	37	Anstow. Gordon-on-Tees	30	6	43	To Denchworth.	
600	21	6	43	Young Mary	Mr T. Young	Stow Hill Childrey	"	29	11	30	Wantage C of E. Girls				Left to Employment. [illegible]	See Previous Register [illegible]
658	"	"	"	Young Francis	" "	" "	"	12	9	33	" " [illegible]	1	5	44	To Wingfield Hospital	See Previous Register, & Page 6.
862	22	6	43	Kimber Paul Michael Prestley	Mr P. Kimber	The Paddocks, Sparsholt	"	13	10	34	Private Tuition	12	8	43	To King Alfred's School.	See re-admission. Page 7.
863	14	9	43	Harris Aubrey Clive	Mr F.J. Harris	Council Houses West Challow	"	8	8	~~38~~	None	29	1	46.	Removed from Register 23.1.46. To Cothill Sanatorium. - Away with glands	Home Address 133 Waye Avenue Cranford Hounslow See Page 6
864	4	10	43	Leck Brian Crawford	Mr Robert C. Leck c/o Mrs Stratton	Bridge Farm West Challow	"	15	4	38	Cranford Hounslow	23	12	43	Returned to Hounslow.	
865	23	10	43	~~[illegible]~~ Groad Raymond	Mr D. Groad	c/o Mrs Groad, The Green, Childrey	"	19	8	37	Sutton Courtenay	28	10	[illegible]	Returned to Sutton Courtenay	
866	4	11	43	Sergeant Sheila	Mr J. Hammond	No 6 Council Houses Childrey	"	8	3	35	Stanford-in-Vale.	26	11	43	Returned to Stanford.	Address 112 Brickmarsh Rd Blackheath. SE 3
703	22	11	43	Harris Sheila Thirza	c/o Mrs Hawtin	No 7 Council Houses Childrey	"	19	3	34	Kidbrook Blackheath	23	4	45	Returned Home	Ditto
798	"	"	"	Harris Eileen Mary	" "	" "	"	31	12	35	" "	"	"	"	Returned Home.	
867	10	1	44	Turner Jacqueline	Mr G. Turner	High St. Childrey	"	7	9	37	Private	10	1	47	To Wantage C of E.	

Admission No. 29	Date of Admission (or Re-Admission) Day	Mon	Year	Full Name of Child	Name of Parent or Guardian	Address	What Exemption, if any, from Religious Instruction is Claimed?	Date of Birth Day	Mon	Year	Name of Last School he Attended before Entering this School. If this is his First School the word "None" must be entered.	Date of Last Attendance at this School Day	Mon	Year	Cause of Leaving	Remarks 29
868	10	1	44	Burls Shirley Ann	Mr R. Burls	Mount Pleasant, Stow Hill Childrey	None	24	3	39	—	29	7	52	To Wantage C of E Senior Dept	
869	10	1	44	Vanderwell Rosemary Stella	Mr H. Vanderwell	16 West St. Childrey	None	7	3	39	—	29	7	52	To Wantage County Senior Dept	
825	13	3	44	Simmons Mary	Mrs C. Cornish	Stow Hill, Childrey	None	21	10	36	Tinnymore Road Junior Mixed Dagenham (Ec).	10	8	44	Returned Home	See also Page [illegible]
662	18	4	44	Bosley Vernon Jack	Mr V. F. Bosley	Cliff Farm East Challow	None	2	11	32	Wantage C of E	8	12	46	Age. – To Employment	See Previous Register
870	18	4	44	Fisher Leonard	c/o Miss Stallon	Bridge Farm West Challow	None	28	11	34	Wandle Park Shepherds Bush W.12.	20	7	43	Returned Home	1 Stanfield Rd. Shepherds Bush W.12.
871	18	4	44	Forshaw John	Mr Henry Forshaw	Westcott Wantage	None	30	3	31	Cafeal School Leatherhead	29	3	45	Age	
797	18	4	44	Brown Patricia Ann	Mr W. P. Brown	c/o Mr Evans West Challow	None	6	1	36	St Sutton School Reading	30	7	47	To Faringdon County Girls	See also Page 3.
872	19	4	44	Howell Sheila	Mrs Howell	c/o [illegible]	None	25	[illegible]	33	Pooles Park Finsbury Park	19	5	44	Returned to Finsbury Park	15 [illegible] Rd. Finsbury Park.
873	24	4	44	Howell Gordon Leonard	Mrs Howell	"	None	4	8	31	Upper Hornsey Rd. Senior School	19	5	44	Returned to Finsbury Park	Do.
864	27	4	44	Leck Brian Crawford	c/o Mrs Stallon	Bridge Farm West Challow	None	15	4	38	Cranford Hounslow	9	6	44	Returned to Hounslow	133 Ways Avenue Cranford Hounslow
874	11	5	44	Leck Patricia Maureen	Do	Do	Do	17	4	39	[illegible]	9	6	44	Returned to Hounslow	Do. See also Page 5
658	15	5	44	Young Francis	Mr F. Young	2 Stow Hill, Childrey	None	12	9	33	Orthopaedic Hospital Wingfield Morris	22	12	48	Age	See Page 5 and Previous Register
743	19	6	44	Simmons Rose	c/o Mrs C. Cornish	3 Stow Hill Childrey	None	18	12	31	Grafton Senior Dagenham	10	8	44	Returned Home	See also Page 1. [illegible]
747	"	"	"	Simmons William John	Do	Do	None	5	9	30	Do	10	8	44	Returned Home	Do. See Also Page 1
875	3	7	44	Halsey Ronald	Sydney Wm. Halsey c/o Mr R. Stallon	Bridge Farm West Challow	None	10	10	33	Wandle Park Coldhall Rd. Shepherds Bush L.C.C.	3	1	45	Returned Home	73 Askew Road Shepherds Bush W.12. Official Evacuee
876	10	7	44	House Sydney Thomas	Mrs A. E. Taylor	White Cottage Childrey	None	29	3	35	Kirby Grove Bermondsey S.E.1 L.C.C.	21	12	44	Returned to Bermondsey	[illegible] Guinness Buildings Bermondsey S.E.1 Official Evacuee L.C.C.
690	10	7	44	Welch Albert Reginald	Mrs Welch	c/o Mr R. Smith Godfrey's Farm Childrey	None	23	5	33	Mitcham Lane Streatham L.C.C.	8	8	44	Returned Home	Unaccompanied Evacuee 203 [illegible] Rd. Streatham S.W.16. See also Previous Register
~~877~~				~~Welch Albert Reginald~~	~~Mrs Welch~~	~~c/o Mr R. Smith, Godfrey's Farm~~	~~None~~	~~24~~	~~5~~	~~33~~	~~Mitcham Lane Streatham L.C.C.~~					
877	"	"	"	Welch Brian Thomas	Mrs Welch	Do	Do	3	9	38	Do. L.C.C.	13	7	44	Returned Home Absent several weeks before	Do.
812	17	7	44	Ralph George	c/o Miss Stallon	Bridge Farm W. Challow	None	17	11	33	Randall St. School Wye St. Battersea S.W.11 L.C.C.	19	1	45	Returned Home	See also Page 3 10 Afghanistan Rd. Battersea S.W.11 L.C.C. (Official Evacuee)
811	"	"	"	Ralph Eileen	c/o Mr R. Stallon	"	"	23	2	32	Do.	19	1	45	Returned Home	See also Page 3. 10 Afghanistan Rd. Battersea S.W.11. L.C.C. (Official Evacuee)
878	"	"	"	Taylor Roy Eric	Mr Frank Taylor c/o Mr W. Panting	Council Houses Childrey	"	26	12	33	Leo St. Peckham	7	3	45	Returned Home	49 Jesson St. [illegible] London S.E.15 (Official Evacuee) L.C.C.
824	"	"	"	Fisher Julia Ann	c/o Mrs J. Hammond	Council Houses Childrey	"	29	10	36	Santley St. Brixton S.W.4 L.C.C.	10	8	44	Returned Home	See also Page 4. 20 Santley St. Brixton L.C.C. (Official Evacuee)
879	24	7	44	Chant Stella Mabel Yvonne Lily	Mr G. Chant c/o Mrs R. Stallon	Bridge Farm W. Challow	"	12	12	35	Cranford, Berkeley St. Hounslow Middlesex	20	7	45	Returned Home	133 Ways Avenue Cranford Hounslow Middx. (Official Evacuee)
880	1	8	44	Wyllie Elspeth	Mrs Elspeth	c/o Mr J. John Council Houses West St Childrey	"	16	9	39	Convent Ursuline of the Sacred Heart [illegible] Kent	10	8	44	To Scotland	60 Farnborough Avenue [illegible] Kent Official Evac.
881	1	8	44	Booker Terrance	Mr H. Booker	High St. Childrey	"	14	12	39	N/L	19	10	49	To Harwell C of E School pro tem.	
755	13	9	44	Short Patricia	c/o Mrs A. Pelleper	Stow Hill Childrey	[illegible]	16	2	35	Tinnymore Rd. Junior Dagenham	6	10	44	Returned to Dagenham	4 Walbrey Gardens Dagenham Essex.
882	2	10	44	Archer Leon Godfrey	Mrs Archer	Mill Farm East Challow	"	14	8	37	East Challow				To Wantage [illegible]	
883	8	1	45	Sale Colin	Mrs G. Lester	Council Houses W. Challow		27	10	34	None	20	7	45	Left Area	
884	"	"	"	Spicer Andrew	Mr Wm. W. Spicer	West Challow		4	11	39		19	12	50	Removed to East Challow C of E	
874	"	"	"	Leck Patricia Maureen	c/o Mrs Stallon	Bridge Farm West Challow		17	4	39	Princes Risboro Schnailds School				Returned Home	Address 133 Ways Avenue Cranford Middx. 49 Bruschamp Rd. S.W.1. See Above
864	"	"	"	Leck Brian Crawford	"			15	4	38	Springwell Road School Heston Middlesex				Returned Home	130 Cranford Lane Heston Middx. See Also Page 5
~~885~~				~~Belcher Alan Kenneth~~	~~Mr Gerald Belcher~~	~~Petwick Cottage Childrey~~		~~8~~	~~6~~	~~33~~						Had been attending Grove & therefore could not be admitted.
885	28	3	45	Ivan John Gibbs	Mr J. Gibbs	Mays Farm [illegible] Challow	None	8	10	35	Upper Stallon	17	2	47	To Faringdon Sec.	Stanswyck Stanstead Cottage Shrivenham
886	"	"	"	Sidney Charles Gibbs				6	9	37		-	-	-	Shrivenham C of E pro tem	
887	-	-	-	Sylvia Mary Gibbs				9	5	39		14	10	46	To Stanford pro tem	

30 | 39

Admission No.	Date of Admission (or Re-Admission) Day	Mon	Year	Full Name of Child	Name of Parent or Guardian	Address	What Exemption, if any, from Religious Instruction is Claimed?	Date of Birth Day	Mon	Year	Name of Last School he attended before entering this School. If this is his first School the word "None" must be entered.	Date of Last Attendance at this School Day	Mon	Year	Cause of Leaving	Remarks
888	10	4	45	Bennett William Harry	Mr H. Bennett	Dog Lane, Childrey	None	7	3	40	None	21	7	53	Transferred to Wantage County School at 13 yrs.	
889	10	5	45	Burbage Francis	Mrs K. [illegible]	c/o Mrs Stratton, Bridge Farm W. Chall.	None	13	11	34	Huntingdon Rd. Council Thrapston. Northants.	20	7	45	Returned Home.	East London School South Park. Sheppards Bush W.12. (Not known)
890	12	9	45	Stratton Jacqueline June	Mr H. Stratton	Bridge Farm, W. Challow	None	19	8	40	None	15	2	46	To: North Hills Farm Long Wellingham 3.46. Away with Kingdom.	
891	17	9	45	Exall Sylvia	Mr T. Exall	Stow Hill, Childrey	None	12	3	36	Hemdean Rd. C. School Reading	2	11	45	To Sparsholt School.	
892	"	"	"	Exall Lesley Lawrence	Mr Tom Exall	" "	"	2	8	36	Do.	2	11	45	" " "	
893	9	1	46	Brown Michael L.	Mr C. Brown	Stow Hill Childrey	None	8	1	41	None.	21	7	54	Transferred to Wantage C. at 13	
894	"	"	"	Burls Barbara Irene	Mr H. Burls	" "	"	3	1	41	"	28	7	54	Transferred to Wantage C at 13	
895	"	"	"	Gibbs Margaret Jessie	Mr J. Gibbs	West Challow	"	5	1	41	"	17	2	47	To Shrivenham C of E from	Stanswick Cottages Shrivenham
896	1	5	46	Gibbs Roger	Mr G. Gibbs	The Crown Inn Childrey	"	7	4	41	"	29	8	52	Removed to Badbury Hill, Fairyard, Nr Swindon	Attending Wroughton S School.
897	"	"	"	Bennett Robert Leslie	Mrs H. Bennett	Stow Hill Childrey	"	12	5	41	"	28	7	54	Transferred to Wantage C at 13.	
898	"	"	"	Collins Michael George	Mr F. Collins	Council Houses Childrey	"	24	5	41	"	28	7	51	Transferred to Wantage C. at 13.	
899				Bailey Ruth Lillian Ann	Mr [illegible] Bailey	Bridge Farm W. Challow	"	7	6	33	[illegible] C of E.	29	7	49	To Wantage C.	
649	12	6	46	Vandervell Dawn	Mr H. Vandervell	Council Houses West St Childrey	None	22	4	33			7	48	Age.	See also Pages 21 and 23 Not [illegible]
825	26	3	46	Simmons Mary Eliz	Mr C. Cornish	West St. Childrey	None	26	10	36	Fanny more Rd. Dagenham Essex.	7	6	46	Returned to Dagenham.	See also Page [illegible]
676	11	9	46	Vandervell Lorna Violet	Mrs H. Vandervell	West St. Childrey	None	26	4	34	Lowe Rd. Council School Wellingham.	13	4	49	Age.	See Pages 21 + 23. [illegible]
900	11	9	46	Gebbard Mervyn Reginald	Mr R.E. Gebbard.	Dog Lane Childrey	None	4	11	41	None.	22	7	55	To Wantage County School at 13+	
901	"		"	Cornish Christopher Robert	Mr Chris Cornish	West St "	None	12	11	41	None.	22	7	55 13+	To Wantage County at 13+	
902	"	"	"	Read Joan Ellen	Mr J.H. Read	Stow Hill "	None	25	4	41	None.	4	12	56 15+	Age.	Absent before end of Term. (19/12/56).
863	23	10	46	Haines Aubrey Clive	Mr F.J. Haines	Council Houses West Challow	None	8	8	38	Coldash Sanatorium	24	7	57 13+	To Wantage County School.	See Page 25 for previous entry.
887	7	1	47	Gibbs Sylvia	Mr J. Gibbs	West Challow	None	9	5	39		17	2	47	To Shrivenham C of E from	See also Page .. Stanswick Cottages Shrivenham
903	15	4	47	Green William Henry ~~Henry Albert~~	Mr Henry Albert Green	West Challow	None	22	10	35	Fairford Glos. Snr. C of E.	3	10	47	Removed to Marlborough Area	
904	"	"	"	Green Ronald Edward	"	" "	"	14	6	37	Wellford Glos.	"	"	"	" " "	
905	"	"	"	Green Gordon John	"	" "	"	16	2	39	" "	"	"	"	" " "	
906	"	"	"	Green Frank Robert	"	" "	"	8	12	41	" "	"	"	"	" " "	
907	"	"	"	Barnard Aubrey Sidney	Mr Albert Barnard	" "	"	29	1	36	Farnborough C of E.	23	3	48	Dudgrove. Nr Fairford Glos.	
908	"	"	"	Barnard June May	" "	" "	"	15	6	40	" "	"	"	"	Ditto	
909	"	"	"	Manser Penelope Jane	Mr R.J. Manser	Dog Lane Childrey	"	13	1	42	None.	25	7	47	Left the District.	
910	"	"	"	Sims Valerie Catherine Yvonne	Mrs C. Sims	West St "	"	22	2	42	"	22	7	55 13+	Transfer to Wantage County at 13+	
850 ~~911~~	"	"	"	Re-admission. Iles Cyril Frederick	Mr C. Iles	Letcombe Bassett.	"	15	11	34	Wantage C of E	29	7	49	To Wantage C.	Re-admission See Page 5
X 911	"	"	"	Hook Michael Richard Edward	Mr F. Button	Sparsholt.	"	3	5	38	Sparsholt	28	3	50	To Mrs R. Pearce. [illegible] Rd. Bristol [illegible] Rubery. Birmingham.	
X 912	"	"	"	Hook Peter Victor Wm.	"	"	"	9	8	39	"	24	7	51	To King Alfred's School Wantage.	
913	"	"	"	Haines Robin Noel	Mr F.J. Haines	West Challow.	"	16	12	41	None	22	7	55	To Wantage County at 13+	
914	21	4	47	Moss Patrick Joseph	Mrs Florence Dillon	High St. Childrey	R C	17	4	39	Private School	30	7	47	To Whatcombe	
915	"	"	"	Hannaby Patricia Mary	Mr J.E. Hannaby	The Forge "	None	22	4	37	Kingston Lisle	20	7	50	Transferred to Wantage County at 13	
916	10	9	47	Legge Jonathan	Mr R.O. Legge Jnr.	High St "	"	22	11	42						

31

Admission No.	Date of Admission (or Re-Admission) Day	Mon	Year	Full Name of Child	Name of Parent or Guardian	Address	What Exemption, if any, from Religious Instruction is Claimed?	Date of Birth Day	Mon	Year	Name of Last School he Attended before Entering this School. If this is his First School the word "None" must be entered.	Date of Last Attendance at this School Day	Mon	Year	Cause of Leaving	Remarks. 31
917	10	9	47	Hook Ronald	Mr F. Bullen	The Stables, Sparsholt Manor	None	15	5	41	Sparsholt C of E	21	7	15+ 54	Transferred to Wantage Coll at 13	
918	15	9	47	Skinner Robert	Mr F. Skinner	8 Council Houses Sparsholt	"	1	5	34	Sparsholt C of E	13	4	15+ 49	Age 15	
919	"	"	"	Bishop Anthony Angelin	Mr R. Bishop	14 " "	"	17	8	34	" "	29	7	15+ 49	Age	
920	"	"	"	Rowland Peter John	Mr A. Rowland	5 " "	"	10	7	34	" "	24	7	49 15+	Age	
921	"	"	"	Skinner Malcolm Ernest	Mr E. Skinner	11 " "	"	2	8	35	" "	29	7	49 14+	Transferred to Wan[illegible]	
922	"	"	"	James George Wm	Mr G. James	9 " "	"	12	4	36	" "	2	7	47	Left the District	
923	"	"	"	Pike Dinah Ruth	Mr J. Pike	Westcot Lane, Westcot	"	28	1	35	" "	30	4	48	Left the District	
924	"	"	"	Pike Louise	Mr W. Pike	" "	"	30	10	34	"		7	48	To Sparsholt	
925	"	"	"	Smith Margaret Rose	Mr E. Smith	Watery Lane Sparsholt	"	28	5	36	" "		7	48	To Sparsholt C of E	
926	"	"	"	Smith Ruth Julia	" "	" "	"	16	7	34	"		7	48	To Sparsholt C of E	
885	29	9	47	Gibbs Ivan John	Mr J. Gibbs	Box Cottage, West Challow	"	8	10	35	Faringdon Sec. Modern; [illegible] C of E	29	7	13+ 49	To Wantage County School	See Page 6
886	"	"	"	Gibbs Sidney Charles	Do.	" " "	"	6	9	37	Shrivenham C of E Do.	24	7	13+ 51	To Wantage County School	Do.
895	"	"	"	Gibbs Margaret	Do		"	5	1	41	Do.	14	1	53	Seven Bridges Farm Cricklade	See Page 7.
927	"	"	"	Gibbs Raymond Kenneth	Mr J. Gibbs	Box Cottage, West Challow	R.C.	23	2	42	Shrivenham C of E	14	12	53	To Seven Bridges Farm, Cricklade.	
928	6	10	47	Betterton Pamela Ann	Mrs J. Betterton	3 Stow Hill, Childrey	R.C.	2	1	40	East Challow C of E	21	7	53	Transferred to Wantage County School at 13 yrs.	
929	"	"	"	Betterton Pauline Julia	"	" "	R.C.	3	10	42	" "	16	9	53	To Grove Ave Farm	
930	"	"	"	Bushrod Graham A.W.	Mr Bushrod	Challow Station	None	14	1	42?	Shellingford C of E	6	10	47	To Sparsholt C of E	
887	13	10	47	Gibbs Sylvia	Mr J. Gibbs	Box Cottage W. Challow	None	3	5	39	Stanford-in-the-Vale	29	7	52 14+	To Wantage County Senior Dept.	See Also Page 6.
931	4	11	47	Broom Roger Walter	Mr E. Broom	West St. Childrey	None	2	1	35	Faringdon Secondary Modern	2	7	48	Returned to Farnham.	
932	7	1	48	Skinner Leonard Ernest	Mr F. Skinner	8 Council Houses Sparsholt	None	23	1	37	Sparsholt C of E	20	7	50 13+	Transferred to Wantage County at 13.	
933	"	"	"	Smith Maureen Ann	Mr G.E. Smith	Council Houses W. St. Childrey	None	2	2	42	Do.	22	7	55 13+	Transfer to Wantage County at 13+	
934	"	"	"	Buchanan Jean	Mr W. Buchanan	West Street Childrey	None	20	4	40	Private	24	7	51 11+	To Faringdon County Girls	
935	"	"	"	Gebbard Janice	Mr R.E. Gebbard	Council Houses West St. Childrey	None	12	"	43	None	20	7	56 12+	To [illegible] Sec. Modern Wantage.	
936	8	1	48	Harris Margaret Joan	Mr E.F. Harris	Manor Flat, Childrey	R.C.	3	7	41	Newport Council Mon. New Tredegar Mon.	20	2	48	26 Penrhyn Terrace New Tredegar, Newport Mon.	
937	1	3	48	Bown Jill Yvonne	Mr F. Bown	Childrey, Wantage	None	17	2	40	Three Cross Council School Wimborne Dorset	22	7	51	To Faringdon County Girls	
938	15	6	48	Brennan Michael Henry	Mr M.M. Brennan	Dog Lane, Childrey	R.C.	15	8	41	East Hanney C of E	13	2	47	To Hanney C of E	c/o Mrs Brennan, The Green E. Hanney.
831	5	7	48	McGregor Graham John	Mr McGregor	Council Houses, Childrey	None	21	10	34	Ewell Sec. Modern Nr Epsom	29	7	49	Transferred to Wantage	See also Page 4.
845	5	7	48	Vandervell Herbert Daniel	Mr H. Vandervell	Council Houses West St. Childrey	None	11	11	37	Lower Rd. Council Hanover Notts	29	7	49 11+	To King Alfred's School	See Also Page 5.
939	8	9	48	Corkery Anthony Richard	Mr R. Corkery	Council Houses Childrey	R.C.	4	9	43	None	22	7	55 12+	To King Alfred's School Wantage	
940	"	"	"	Betterton Jerome (Jeremy) John	Mr P.J. Betterton	Stow Hill, Childrey	R.C.	18	11	43	None	16	9	53	To Grove Ave Farm	
941	"	"	"	Rolfe Raymond James	Mr H.J. Rolfe	High St. Childrey	None	8	10	43	None	14	10	49	Left District To Denbigh, N. Wales.	
942	"	"	"	Line James Wm	Mr L.H. Line	Watery Lane Sparsholt	None	28	8	43	None	29	7	49	To Gordon.	
943	"	"	"	Brickell Roger	Mr J.W. Brickell	Broadleaze Farm	None	12	6	43	None	29	7	49	Removed to Ferndale Road, Swindon.	
944	"	"	"	Evans Richard Frank	Mr E. Evans	Watery Lane	None	6	8	37	Sparsholt C of E	29	7	49 14+	To King Alfred's School.	
945	28	9	48	Brennan Maureen Mary	Mrs M. Brennan	Dog Lane Childrey	R.C.		7	43		5	5	49	To East Hanney.	

Admission No.	Date of Admission (or Re-Admission) Day	Mon	Year	Full Name of Child	Name of Parent or Guardian	Address	What Exemption, if any, from Religious Instruction is Claimed?	Date of Birth Day	Mon	Year	Name of Last School he attended before entering this School. If this is his first School the word "None" must be entered.	Date of Last Attendance at this School Day	Mon	Year	Cause of Leaving	Remarks
946	8	11	48	Pert Ian Kenneth	Mr R. Pert	Fernleigh West Challow	None	14	4	43	None	22	7	55 11+	To Faringdon Secondary Modern School	
947	11	1	49	Gibbard Rodney	Mr R.E. Gibbard	12 West St. Childrey	None	5	4	44	"	20	7	56 12+	To Schnield Sec. Modern Sesy. Wantage	
948	31	1	49	Haslam Ian Michael	Mrs N. Haslam	c/o Mrs J. Booker Stow Hill	None	20	12	43	"				To Canal Zone. Father Serving soldier	See also Page 9 below
949	21	3	49	Hay Colin William	Mr Wm. P. Hay	East Manton Stables, Sparsholt	"	4	10	37	Thetford County Primary Norfolk	10	2	50	Left District	Rowan Tree House London Rd. Royston Herts
950	"	"	"	Hay Keith Victor	"	"	"	10	10	40	"	10	2	50	"	"
951	"	"	"	Hay Roy Dennis	"	"	"	3	8	42	"	10	2	50	"	"
952	3	5	49	Bown Brenda Maureen	Mr F.W. Bown	Hatchet Lane Childrey	"	6	5	44		22	7	56 11+	To Faringdon County Girls	
953	"	"	"	Moulford Susan Mary	Mr R. Moulford	Church St. "	"	9	2	44		17	5	55	To West Hendred	
954	"	"	"	Pert Philippa May	Mr R. Pert	Fernleigh, West Challow	"	17	5	44		22	7	55	To St Andrew's Private School Wantage	
955	"	"	"	Bosley Carol	Mr V.F. Bosley	Mill Farm E. Challow	"	15	9	43		20	7	56 12+	To Schnield Sec. Modern Wantage	
956	"	"	"	Burls John Herbert	Mr H. Burls	Stow Hill, Childrey	"	23	6	44		20	7	56 11+	To Schnield Sec. Modern Wantage	
908	"	"	"	Barnard June May	Mr A. Barnard	West Challow	"	15	4	40		21	7	53 13+	Transferred to Wantage County at 13yrs.	See Also Page 7
957	4	5	49	Brennan Margaret	Mr M.M. Brennan	Dog Lane Childrey	"	25	5	44		5	5	49	To Hanney	
958	7	9	49	Smith Eileen Joyce	Mr G.C. Smith	C. Houses West St. Childrey	"	3	10	44		20	7	56 11+	To Faringdon County School	
959	"	"	"	Brown Peter John	Mr C. Brown	"	"	5	11	44		20	7	56 11+	To Schnield Sec. Modern Wantage	
960	"	"	"	Wilkinson Susan Elizabeth Tabor	Mr Thomas J. Wilkinson	c/o Mrs Simmons, Orchard Brink, High St. Childrey	"	2	11	45		20	7	56	To Faringdon County School	Under care of Mother Edna Rosemary
961	"	"	"	Froud Graham Philip	Mr P. Froud	High St. Childrey	"	3	9	44		20	7	56 11+	To Swindon High School	
962	"	"	"	Ellis Peter Michael	Mrs J. Ellis	C. Houses, West St. Childrey	"	29	11	44		20	7	56 11+	To Schnield Sec. Modern Wantage	
963	"	"	"	Bull Margaret Ann	Mrs E. Bull	" " "	"	3	10	44		20	7	56 11+	To Faringdon County School	
964	"	"	"	Read Carole Ann	Mr J.H. Read	" " "	"	11	11	44		20	7	56 11+	To Schnield Sec. Modern Wantage	
965	"	"	"	Smith Gordon William	Mr Smith	Sparsholt	"	24	9	38	Sparsholt C of E	28	9	50	To Walcot Manor Farm Swindon	Believed to be attending Old Town Junior School Swindon
966	"	"	"	Booker Julian	Mrs V.J. Booker	8 C. Houses, The Crescent Childrey	"	17	8	44		20	7	56 11+	To Schnield Sec. Modern Wantage	
967	"	"	"	Hay Derek	Mr Wm. P. Hay	East Manton Stable Sparsholt	"	3	8	44		10	2	50	Left District	Rowan Tree House London Rd. Royston Herts
881	21	11	49	Booker Terrance	Mrs H. Booker	West St. Childrey	None	14	12	39	Returned from Harwell County Primary	24	7	51	To King Alfred's School Wantage	See also Page 6
968	7	9	49	St Pier Marion H.	Mr St. Pier	Stow Hill, Childrey	"	11	12	44		22	1	54	Removed to East Hanney	
969	25	4	50	Whelpdale John S.	Mr J. Whelpdale	West St. Childrey	"	16	4	45		20	7	56 11+	To Schnield Sec. Mod. Wantage	
970	"	"	"	Smith John Richard	Mr R.J. Smith	Godfreys Farm Childrey	"	25	2	45		20	7	56 11+	To Schnield Sec. Mod. Wantage	
971	"	"	"	Middleton Christopher R.	Mr J. Middleton	College Farm Cottages	"	24	4	45					To Redlands School Reading	
972	7	9	50	Elliott Richard Richard	Mrs Elliott	High St. Childrey	"	4	9	45		23	7	57 11+	To Schnield Sec. Modern Wantage	
911	"	"	"	Hook Michael Edward	Mr F. Ruelton	Manor Flat Sparsholt	"	3	5	38	Returned from Farringdon [illegible] on Long Leave. Parents serving with H.M. Forces	24	7	51 13+	To Wantage County School	See also Page 7
948	20	9	50	Haslam Ian Michael	Mrs F. Haslam	c/o Mrs E. Booker Stow Hill, Childrey	"	20	12	43	in Suez Canal Zone The Garrison School [illegible]	19	12	50	Returned to Suez Canal Zone	See also Above
973	"	"	"	Haslam Adrian Leslie	"	"	"	9	10	45	None	19	12	50	Ditto	
974	9	1	51	Palmer David William	Mrs. P. Palmer	The Grotto, Childrey	"	27	1	46		23	7	57 11+	To Schnield Sec. Modern Wantage	
975	"	"	"	Smith Leslie John	Mr. Smith	The Old Manor, West St. Childrey	"	24	10	45		21	3	52	Removed to Drayton	
976	9	1	51	Borgest Allegra Marie St Pere	Mrs. Constance Violet Borgest; Mr. Louis Andrew Henri	Orchard House, Childrey	"	8	9	42	Sparsholt C of E	10	6	51	Removed to 3 Hill Road Chirg, Totton, Southampton	

Admission No. 33	Date of Admission (or Re-Admission) Day	Mon	Year	Full Name of Child	Name of Parent or Guardian	Address	What Exemption, if any, from Religious Instruction is Claimed?	Date of Birth Day	Mon	Year	Name of Last School he attended before entering this School. If this is his first School the word "None" must be entered.	Date of Last Attendance at this School Day	Mon	Year	Cause of Leaving	Remarks 33
977	9	1	51	Borgeest Adrienne Ann	of C.V. Borgeest	Orchard House, Childrey	NIL	22	11	44	Sparsholt C of E	20	4	51	Removed to 4 Nine Rd Eling, Totton Southampton	
978	5	2	51	Winterbourne Patricia Ann	of Mr F. Winterbourne	West St Childrey	NIL	1	5	42	Wantage County Primary	21	3	51	Returned to Wantage.	Mr Walter Winterbourne (Read)
979	6	2	51	Jackson Valerie Millicent Jane	Mr Wm Fred. Jackson	Stow Hill "	NIL	1	3	38	Hutton-in-the-Marsh.	24	7	51 11+	To Wantage County School	
980	"	"	"	Jackson David George	" " "	" " "	"	4	9	39	" " "	19	10	51	To Highworth, Wilts	
981	"	"	"	Jackson ~~William~~ Peter John	" " "	" " "	"	10	8	42	Broadway (Worcs)	"	"	"	To Highworth "	
982	5	3	51	Brown Geoffrey Wallis	Mr V. Borgeest ~~Brown~~	c/o Mrs Borgeest. Orchard House Childrey	"	22	8	45	Infants Central School Southampton	6	3	51	Returned to Southampton	7 Clifford St Southampton.
983	12	4	51	Simmonds Ivy Kathy Ellen	Mrs C. Cornish	West St. Childrey.	NIL	7	6	45	Fanshawe Rd. Junior Dagenham.	24	7	51	Returned to Dagenham.	
984	12	4	51 ~~46~~	Corkery Margaret Therese	Mr R. Corkery	" "	R.C.	6	4	46	NIL	6	3	53	Transferred to Wantage C of E School 6.4.53	
985	12	4	51	Collins David Wm.	Mr P. Collins	Chapel Way Childrey	NIL	4	4	46	NIL	23	7	57 11+	To Icknield Sec. Modern Wantage.	
986	19	6	51	Gebbard Keith.	Mr R.E. Gebbard	West St. Childrey	NIL	19	6	46	NIL	23	7	57 11+	To Icknield Sec. Modern Wantage	
971	30	4	51	Middleton Christopher	Mr J. Middleton	East Challow	NIL	24	4	45	East Challow C of E	18	5	51	Returned to East Challow	See Page 9.
855	21	5	51	Williams Raymond Edward	Mr W. Williams	West St Childrey	NIL.	28	1	38	Lockinge Kent, Boys Nation School, Upm...	24	7	51 13+	To Wantage County ~~Boys~~ School	See Also Page 5.
971	16	7	51	Middleton Christopher	Mr J. Middleton	East Challow.	NIL	24	4	45	East Challow C of E	24	7	51	Returned to E. Challow	See Above & Page 9
987	4	9	51	Richens Michael John	Mr H. Richens	High St. Childrey	NIL.	7	10	46	Nil	23	7	58 11+	Icknield	
988	"	"	"	Gibbs Pamela Rose.	Mr J. Gibbs	West Challow.	NIL	7 ~~23~~	11 ~~X~~	46 ~~44~~	NIL	4	12	53	Seven Bridges Farm. Cricklade.	
989	"	"	"	Taylor David Compton Geoffrey	Mrs R.A. Taylor	West St Childrey	NIL.	18	"	46	NIL	23	7	58 11+	King Alfreds ~~Icknield~~	
990	"	"	"	Gorham Phillip Wm.	Mr Francis Eric Gorham	Clements Cottages Sparsholt.	NIL.	4	9	46.	NIL.	"	"	" 11+	- - -	
991.	"	"	"	James Wendy Florence	Mr Ronald Raymond James	Manor Farm Cottage W. Challow	"	13	6	43	Stanford-in-the-Vale.	20	12	51	To East Challow C of E	
992	"	"	"	James Sylvia Jessie	" " "	" " " "	"	23	"	44	" " "	"	"	"	To East Challow C of E	
993	10	9	51	Button Freda Nancy	Mr F. Button	Manor Flat, Sparsholt	"	21	8	44	Sparsholt C of E.	20	7	56 12+	To Icknield Sec. Modern Wantage.	
994	26	9	51	Steers Allan.	Mr S. Steers	2 West St. Sparsholt.	"	23	3	40	" "	24	7	53 13+	Transferred to Wantage County at 13yrs.	
995	13 ~~1~~	11 ~~1~~	51 ~~52~~	Hardy Michael John P.	Mr Robert Hardy	Stow Hill, Childrey	"	8	10	45	Lambourne	11	7	52.	Removed to	
996	26	4	51	Sherriff John Robert Donald	Mr John D. Sherriff	4 Watery Lane Sparsholt	"	24	6	41	Lee Common Gt Missenden, Bucks.	28	1	52	To Quenington Near Cirencester Attending Hatherop C of E School	
997	"	"	"	Sherriff Angela	" "	" "	"	30	4	43	" "	29	1	52	To Quenington Near Cirencester Att. Hatherop C of E School	
~~999~~ 989	8	1	52	Buchanan Peter	Mr Buchanan		"	10	12	46	None	13	7	55	Left District.	
1000 ~~999~~	"	"	"	Mill Derek	Mr Mill	Dog Lane, Childrey	"	3	1	47	None	20	12	55	To Letcombe Regis	
1001	"	"	"	Du Barry Colin	Mr Du Barry	Sparsholt	"	1	2	45	Sparsholt C of E.	18	1	52	Left ~~=~~ District.	
1002	29	1	52	Matthews Patricia	Mr Henry C. Matthews	College Farm Cottages.	"	4	10	46.	None.	"	2	52	To East Challow C of E.	
998	27	11	51	Sherriff Mary Ann Rosalie	Mr John D Sherriff.	4 Watery Lane Sparsholt	"	24	6	41.	Lee Common Gt. Missenden Bucks.	29	1	52	To Quenington. Nr Cirencester Attending Hatherop C of E School	
1003	22	4	52	Smith Veronica June.	Mr G.C. Smith	West St. Childrey.	"	28	6	47		23	7	58	Icknield	
1004	"	"	"	Rowland Anthony John	Mr A. Rowland	Height "	"	4	6	47		23	7	58	Icknield	
1005	"	"	"	Males Peter Melvin	Mr H. Males	" " "	"	20	3	47.		23	7	58	Icknield	
948	27	5	52	Haslam Ian Michael	Mrs N Haslam (mother)	Child of Mrs John Stow Hill Childrey	"	20	12	43	St John Rushpool School	18	5	53	Left District	Converted from Egyptian Garrison - Tel el Kebir See Page 9
973	"	"	"	Haslam Adrian Leslie	" "	Child of Mrs Vanmuree Chapel Way	"	9	10	45	" "	21	5	53	Left District	" " " "
1006	9	6	52	Wixey Penelope Julia	Mr H. Wixey	High St. Childrey	"	1	7	47	None	9	12	52	To Wantage Primary County	

Admission No.	Date of Admission (or Re-Admission) Day	Mon	Year	Full Name of Child	Name of Parent or Guardian	Address	What Exemption, if any, from Religious Instruction is claimed?	Date of Birth Day	Mon	Year	Name of Last School he attended before entering this School. If this is his first School the word "None" must be entered.	Date of Last Attendance at this School Day	Mon	Year	Cause of Leaving	Remarks
																See also Pages 9 and 10.
971	14	7	52	Meddleton Christopher	Mr J. Meddleton	East Challow. Wantage.	Nil	24	4	45	East Challow.	29	7	52	Returned to East Challow C of E.	Staying temporarily at Post Office, Childrey.
1007	21	7	52	Andrews David Guy	Mrs N Andrews	c/o Mrs R.O. Iles Post Office Childrey	Nil	24	9	46	Alfred Sutton Primary School. Wokingham Road Reading.	29	7	52	Returned to Reading	Parents' address 72 Upper Redlands Rd. Reading
1008	"	"	"	Andrews Graham Grenville	" "		"	"	"	"		19	7	52	" " "	
1009	2	9	52	Culley Angela Jean	Mrs B. Culley	Council Houses, Chapel Way Childrey	"	9	12	47	None	16	10	53	To Sparsholt C of E	
1010	"	"	"	Button Ruth Janet	Mr F Button	Manor Flat. Sparsholt.	"	27	1	46	Sparsholt C of E.	23	7	57 11+	To Icknield Sec. Mod. Wantage	
1011	"	"	"	Corkery Seán Martin	Mr R. Corkery	Council Houses. West St. Childrey	R.C.	10	9	47	None	22	7	59 11+	To Icknield	
1012	"	"	"	Prendergast Barry	Mr P. Prendergast.	" " Chapel Way "	Nil.	29	8	47	None		7		To East Challow C of E.	
1013	"	"	"	Smith Robert Ardley	Mr R. Smith	Church St. Childrey	"	29	9	47	None				Left District.	
1014	"	"	"	Stone Anthony Kevin	Mr W.C. Stone.	East Challow	"	7	6	47	None.	25	6	53	Attending Grove C of E.	
1015	3	9	52	O'Neill Patrick	Capt. R.P. O'Neill R.A.	Beckett Hall, Military College of Science Shrivenham / Manor Flat - Sparsholt.	"	1	12	45	Sparsholt C of E.	28	10	53	Admitted to Telford Primary School 2/11/53 - Surrey P.C.	
1016	15	9	52	Burnage Joyce Muriel	Mr Jack Burnage.	31 Union St. Bedford	"	8	10	42	Clapham Road Bedford.	21	10	52	Returned home to Bedford.	c/o Mr P. Collins Chapel Way, Childrey
1017	22	9	52	Brewer Jacqueline Vera Mary	Mr Thos. Regd. Brewer	The Crown Inn Childrey	"	30	10	47	Mrs Coffin Private School Wantage.	22	7	59 11+	Icknield	
1018	3	11	52	Iles David	Mr J. ILES	Hill Farm "	"	7	5	"	Burbage Wilts	3	6	54	To Randal Cremer County Primary Shoreditch E.2	
1019	"	"	"	Iles Paul		"	"	5	2	47	" "	25	5	54	To Randal Cremer County Primary Shoreditch E.2	Absent ill before final removal.
1020	6	1	53	Williams Jeffrey	Mrs W Williams	12. West St. Childrey	"	5	2	48	None.	22	7	59 11+	Icknield	
1021	"	"	"	Gorham Maureen	Mr Francis Eric Gorham	Clements Cottages, Sparsholt	"	19	2	48	"	22	7	59 11+	Faringdon	
1022	2	2	53	Neville Carole Patricia	Mr B Neville	Manor Flat Childrey	"	7	12	42	Winkfield	13	3	53	Left District	Returned later to Auckland.
1023	"	"	"	Neville Kenneth James		" "	"	7	10	40	"	13	3	53	" "	Returned later to Auckland.
1024	25	2	53	Charlton-Dewar Sandra Clare	1st Bn. Queen's Own Cameron Highlanders Major Wm Charlton-Dewar	High St Childrey	"	23	3	48	None.	10	12	53	Left District.	
1025	14	4	53	Bartlet Sandra	Mr Bartlett.	West Challow	"	29	4	48	None	10	7	53	Removed to Newbury.	
1026	"	"	"	Hannaby John	Mr J. Hannaby	Dog Lane Childrey	"	27	2	48	None	22	7	59 11+	Icknield	
1027	"	"	"	Gasston Ernest William	Mr Gasston	The Grotto, Childrey	"	10	5	48	None.	11	9	53	To R.A.F. Station Gruppen 2nd T.A.F. B.A.O.R. 34.	
1028	12	5	53	O'Neill Christine	Mr R.P. O'Neill	Manor Flat. Sparsholt	"	15	7	47	Sparsholt C of E.	28	10	53	Admitted to Telford Primary School 2/11/53. Surrey S.C.	
1029	8	6	53	Smith Mary Susan	c/o Mrs Brewer.	Crown Inn. Childrey	"	19	4	47	St. Mark's School, Mitcham.	19	6	53	Returned Home.	
1030	6	7	53	Palmer Ann.	Mrs E.H. Palmer	c/o Mrs Palmer, The Grotto, Childrey	"	6	12	47	Sambridge C of E Nr Melksham	21	7	53	Returned to Melksham.	
1031	7	7	53	Scarrott Michael Frederick	Mr Frederick Scarrott.	Caravan, Hatchet Close. Childrey	"	24	12	40	Barrington Glos	13	7	53	Removed to Longcott	Travelling Show People
1032	-	-	-	Scarrott ~~Mabel~~ Maybell Eliz.	—		"	7	3	42	—	14	7	53	" " "	
1033	-	-	-	Scarrott Doreen Edna	Mr George			18	12	41		"	"	"	" "	
1034	1	9	53	Gibbard Marilyn Eliz.	Mr R.E. Gibbard	West St. Childrey	None	22	8	48	None		7	60 11+	Icknield	
1035	"	"	"	Burls Wendy Edna	Mr H. Burls	Mount Pleasant, Stow Hill, Childrey	"	8	10	48	None		7	60	Icknield	
1036	"	"	"	Kendall Paul	Mr A. Kendall	West St. Childrey	"	13	5	48	None	22	7	59 11+	Icknield	
1037	"	"	"	Buchanan Paul Graeme	Mr A. Buchanan	" "	"	30	9	48	None	13	7	55	Left District.	
1038	"	"	"	Mill Dennis Raymond	Mr D.R. Mill	Dog Lane "	"	6	9	48	None	"	12	55	To Letcombe Regis	
1039	"	"	"	Aldridge James John	Mr A. Aldridge	High St "	"	8	10	48	None		7	60 11+	Icknield	
1040	"	"	"	Acton Raymond George	Mr G.F. Acton	Stow Hill "	"	3	10	48	None				?	
1041	"	"	"	Bishop Raymond William	Mr R. Bishop		"	21	5	44	Sparsholt	20	7	56 11+	To Icknield Sec. Mod. Wantage.	

35

Admission No.	Date of Admission (or Re-Admission) Day	Mon	Year	Full Name of Child	Name of Parent or Guardian	Address	What Exemption, if any, from Religious Instruction is Claimed?	Date of Birth Day	Mon	Year	Name of Last School he Attended before entering this School. If this is his first School the word "None" must be entered.	Date of Last Attendance at this School Day	Mon	Year	Cause of Leaving	Remarks
929	28	9	53	Betterton Pauline Julia	Mrs P. J. Betterton	Stow Hill Childrey	None	3	10	42	Grove - Pro. Tem.	17	11	55	To Portsmouth Area	See Also Page 8.
940	"	"	"	Betterton Jeremy John	" "	" " "	"	18	10	43	" " "	17	11	55	" " "	See Also Page 8.
1042	19	10	53	Vaughan Frances Clare	Mrs H.D. Vaughan	High St. Childrey	"	7	1	45	St. Annes R.C. Caversham	20	7	58 11+	To Cath. School of Our Lady. Sec. School Abingdon	
1043	"	"	"	Vaughan Gerard Gilbert Anthony	" "	" "	"	26	3	48	" " "	22	7	59 11+	King Alfred's	
1044	3	11	53	Vaughan Adrian Hugh	" "	" "	"	10	1	41	Alfred Sutton, Sec. Mod. Reading	28	7	54 13+	Transferred to Wantage County at 13.	
1009	9	11	53	Culley Angela	Mrs B Culley	12 Chapel Way Childrey	"	9	12	47	From Sparsholt C of E.	25	1	54	To Stanford in the Vale Mother taken to hospital.	See Also Page 11
1045	7	1	54	Rowland Pauline Lesley	Mr A. Rowland.	High St. Childrey	"	8	4	49			7	60 11+	Icknield	
1046	"	"	"	Vowles Josephine Janet Stephanie	Mr J Vowles	West St. "	"	25	4	49		1	9	56	To Fawley School Returned to Keighley.	
1047	"	"	"	Atkinson Pamela Kathleen	Mr Atkinson	High St. Childrey	"	17	1	47	Ingrow Infants. Keighley Yorks.	26	1	54	Left District	Home Pro. Tem. c/o Mrs J. Symonds. High St. Childrey
1014	"	"	"	Stone Anthony Kevin	Mr W. C. Stone	The Pen Mill, East Challow	"	7	6	47	Grove C of E.	23	7	58 11+	Icknield	See Also Page. 11.
1015	30	11	53	O'Neill Patrick	Captn R.P. O'Neill R.A.	Manor Flat, Sparsholt Beckett Hall, Military College of Science	R.C.	1	12	45		18	3	54	Left District	See Page. 11. Original Admission
1028	"	"	"	O'Neill Christine	" " "	" " "	R.C.	15	7	47		12	3	54	" "	See Page 11. Original Admission.
1048	11	1	54	Iles Pauline Margaret Rose.	Mr J Iles	Hill Barn. Sparsholt	None.	10	1	49	None	3	6	54	To Randal Cremer County Primary Shoreditch E. 2.	
1049	26	1	54	Toms Janet Lucy	Mr Chas Horace Toms	King Charles Cottage.	None.	28	3	45	Barford St. Martin. Nr Salisbury Wilton	9	4	54	Left District	
1053 [redacted]	22	3	54	Cross Leslie George.	Mr F Cross -	Grove. c/o Mrs Betterton 2a Chapel Way Childrey	None	21	11	44	Grove.	13	4	54	Returned to Grove.	
1050	8	2	54	Balfe David William	Mr Wm. Balfe	Stow Hill Childrey	Tions	27	4	45	Weddington, Essex	20	7	58 11+	To Wantage Icknield Sec. Modern Wantage	
1051	"	"	"	Balfe Bernadette Margaret	" "	" " "	"	18	7	46	"	17	9	54	To ~~Icknield Sec. Modern Wantage~~ Unknown	See Also Page 13. Parents separated
1052	"	"	"	Beasant Robert James	Mr R J Beasant	Challow Marsh Farm	"	25	9	45	Dorchester	23	7	57	To Icknield Sec. Modern Wantage.	
1054	27	4	54	Allsop Alan	Mr H Allsop	King Charles Cottage, Childrey	"	4	11	42	Torriano Avenue Kentish Town, St. Pancras		7	55 13+	To King Alfred's School Wantage.	Reported for admission on 27.4.54. Owing to illness of Staff children had to return home.
1055	"	"	"	Allsop Elaine	"	" " " "	"	4	11	42	Ditto	17	12	54 12+	To Yorkshire	
1056	"	"	"	Allsop George	"	" " " "	"	27	8	45	Ditto	"	"	"	"	
1057	"	"	"	Allsop Brenda	"	" " "	"	2	3	47	Ditto	"	"	"	"	
1009	"	"	"	Culley Angela	Mrs B Culley	12 Chapel Way Childrey	"	9	12	47	From Stanford in the Vale		7	59 11+	Icknield	See Above + Page 11
1058	19	7	54	Cullen Michael Olivier	Mr S. Cullen	West St. Childrey	R.C.	12	1	43	Kilbride Nr Dublin	20	7	56 13+	To Icknield Sec. Modern Wantage.	
1059	"	"	"	Cullen Thomas	" "	" "	"	14	4	44	" "	20	7	56 12+	To Icknield Sec. Modern Wantage.	
1060	"	"	"	Cullen James	" "	" "	"	31	7	46	" "	20	7	56 11+	To Icknield Sec. Modern Wantage.	
971	29	8	54	Middleton Christopher	Mr S Middleton	Chapel Way Childrey	None	24	4	45	East Challow	20	7	56 11+	To King Alfred's School Wantage.	See Also Pages 9, 10 and 11.
1061	31	8	54	Smith Susan Mary	Mr G.C. Smith	West St. "	"	15	11	49	None		7	61 11+	Icknield	
1062	"	"	"	Culley Sandra Pauline	Mr B. Culley	12 Chapel Way "	"	25	8	49	"		7	61 11+	Faringdon	
1063	"	"	"	Young Marion	Mr W. Young	22 Chapel Way "	"	16	9	49	"		7	61 11+	Icknield	
1064	"	"	"	Cecil Christie	Mr L. Cecil	" West Challow	"	9	10	49	"	27	5	55	Returned to America	American Service Man. Born in San Francisco Califor.
1029	"	"	"	Smith Susan Mary	Mrs Smith c/o Mrs Brewer	Crown Inn, Childrey	"	9	4	47	St Mark's School Mitcham		?		Returned Home	See Also Page 11
1065	31	8	54	Parry Belle Anita	Mrs Elkin Parry	No 4 Stow Hill Childrey	"	7	11	49		30	3	56	To Grove.	
1066	4	1	55	Froud Diane Bertha Margaret	Mr P. Froud	Orchard Drive, Childrey.	"	6	1	50		23	7	58	To St. Andrews Wantage	
1067	3	11	49	Smith Norman	Mrs Helen A. Smith	Coppice Leaze West Challow	"	3	12	49			7	61 11+	Icknield	

Admission No. 36	Date of Admission (or Re-Admission) Day	Mon	Year	Full Name of Child	Name of Parent or Guardian	Address	What Exemption, if any, from Religious Instruction is Claimed?	Date of Birth Day	Mon	Year	Name of Last School he attended before entering this School. If this is his first School the word "None" must be entered.	Date of Last Attendance at this School Day	Mon	Year	Cause of Leaving	Remarks 36
1068	19	4	55	Rowland Leslie	Mr R. Rowland	No 26 Chapel Way	None	24	6	50	None		7	61	Icknield	
1069	〃	〃	〃	Rowland Christine Linda	Mr K. Rowland	No 4 Chapel Way	None	29	5	50	None		7	61	Faringdon	
1070	6	6	55	Janesch Stephen	Mr Duncan Janesch	High St. Childrey	None	12	12	47	St Andrews Private School Wantage	20	12	55	To Abingdon.	Had attended Tidworth C of E
1029	6	6	55	Smith Susan Mary	Mrs Smith c/o Mrs Brewer	Crown Inn, Childrey	None	19	4	47	Alfred Mizen Pollards Hill Mitcham	10	6	55	Returned Home. ?	See Also Pages 11 and 12.
1071	6	9	55	Axton Patricia Anne	Mr G. F. Axton	Stow Hill, Childrey, Wantage.	〃	27	11	50	None.					
1072	〃	〃	〃	Breakspear Sandra	Mr F. Breakspear	Chapel Way, Childrey	〃	3	7	50	〃				Removed to Private School	
1073	〃	〃	〃	Burls Susan Jane	Mr H. Burls	Stow Hill 〃	〃	31	10	50	〃					
1074	〃	〃	〃	England Julie Susan	Mr England	Chapel Way 〃	〃	31	10	50	〃					
1075	〃	〃	〃	Simmonds Marilyn Ann	Mr L. Simmonds	〃 〃 〃	〃	12	12	50	〃				Left district —	Gaston Lane C.P.
~~1076~~	~~〃~~	~~〃~~	~~〃~~	~~Parry Jill Anita~~	~~Mr E. Parry~~	~~Stow Hill~~		7	11	49	〃					
1076	〃	〃	〃	Cox Victor Kenneth	Mr J. Cox	West Challow	〃	4	5	50	〃		7	61	Icknield	
1077	12	9	55	Quennell Julia Ann	Mr J. Quennell	The Caravan Childrey	〃	3	7	47	Upper Fairham Road Romford	14	2	56.	Left District Hermitage?	
1051	6	9	55	Balfe Jornadette M	Mr Balfe	Stow Hill, Childrey	RC	18	7	46		23	7	57	To Icknield Sec. Modern Wantage.	
1078	3	10	55	Spares Stuart George	Mr C. W. Spares	Stow Hill Childrey	None	7	9	46	Shepreth Village School Cambs.	14	6	57	Thorpe. Mr Tamworth Staffs	
1079	〃	〃	〃	Spares Charles Wm	〃 〃	〃	None	14	4	44	Sawston Village College Cambs.	30	7	56	To Icknield Sec. Modern Wantage. ?	
1027	1	12	55	Gasston Ernest William	Mr Gasston	c/o The Grotto 〃	None	20	5	48	B.F.E.S. School R.A.F. Station, Brueggen, BAOR.					
1080	12	1	56	Hague Douglas	Mrs Hague	The Caravan, Stow Hill Childrey	None	9	7	50	None	20	7	57	To East Challow C of E	
1081	18	4	56	Floyd Linda	Mr R. J. Floyd	25 Chapel Way, Childrey	None	4	6	51	None.					
1082	〃	〃	〃	Cullen Richard	Mr J. Cullen	West Street Childrey	R.C.	24	6	51	None	20	7	56	To Letcombe.	
1083	〃	〃	〃	Males Stuart John	Mr H. Males	High Street Childrey	None	4	4	51	None					
1084	23	5	56	Harris Keith Leonard	Mr E. Harris	The Green Childrey	None	26	2	49	Sparsholt Cont.	1	10	58	Removed to Letcombe —	School Wantage C.E. Boys
1085	5	9	58	Seay Marilyn Marie	Mr Charles Clyde Seay	Dog Lane Childrey	None	24	5	51	None.		12	56	Left District	American Service Man
1086	〃	〃	〃	Corkery Bridget Mary	Mr R. Corkery	West St. 〃	R.C.	5	3	51	None.					
1087	〃	〃	〃	Rowland Deborah Elsie	Mr E. R. Rowland	Station Rd. 〃	None	7	12	51	None.					
1029	〃	〃	〃	Smith Susan Mary	c/o Mrs Brewer	Crown Inn Childrey	None.	19	4	47	Alfred Mizen Pollards Hill Mitcham	14	9	47	Returned Home.	
1088	〃	〃	〃	Palmer Susan	c/o Mrs Palmer Elaine	The Grotto Childrey	None	19	12	48		19	12	55	Returned Home.	
1089	25	9	56	Kingsman Andrew	Mr L. E. Elliott	Symmonds Farm Childrey	None	2	8	45	St. Jumalos, Oxford	28	6	57	To Dunmow Essex.	
1090	〃	〃	〃	Kingsman Miles	〃	〃 〃 〃	〃	23	9	46	〃 〃	28	6	57	To Dunmow, Essex.	The Bungalow, Moor End, Great Dunmow, Essex. Attending Grammar School.
1091	〃	〃	〃	Kingsman Paul	〃	〃 〃 〃	〃	17	1	48	〃 〃	28	6	57	Removed to Dunmow Essex.	
1092	9	10	56	Kingsman Rodney Richard	〃	〃 〃 〃	〃	21	9	50	〃 〃	28	6	57	To Dunmow Essex.	
1093	29	10	56	Wheeler Susan Joyce	Mr J. Wheeler	Church St. Childrey	〃	9	9	46	Swanbourne Bucks.	23	7	58	Icknield	[illegible]
1094	〃	〃	〃	Wheeler Jennifer Margaret	〃	〃 〃	〃	4	5	48	Swanbourne, Bucks	22	7	59	Icknield	
1096	15	1	57	Davies Michael	Mr R. J. Davies	Childrey House	〃	6	1	48	St. Peters Droitwich	25	3	59	Transferred to special school	
1097	〃	〃	〃	Davies Christina Frances	〃	〃 〃	〃	12	1	50	〃 〃				Left District	
1095	8	1	57	Legge Sally Patricia	Mr R. Legge	High St. Childrey	〃	15	4	52	None					
1098	22	1	57	Baker Geoffrey Charles	Mr R. J. Baker	Yeor Cottage, West St. Childrey	〃	20	5	46	Gradenstoke Wilts	23	7	57	To Icknield Sec. Modern Wantage.	

Admission No. 37	Date of Admission (or Re-Admission) Day	Mon	Year	Full Name of Child	Name of Parent or Guardian	Address	What Exemption, if any, from Religious Instruction is Claimed?	Date of Birth Day	Mon	Year	Name of Last School he attended before entering this School. If this is his first School the word "None" must be entered.	Date of Last Attendance at this School Day	Mon	Year	Cause of Leaving	Remarks 37
1099	20	2	57	Tucker Gillian Suzanne	Mr Wm Tucker	High St. Childrey.	None	25	11	47	East Bridgford J.M.I. C of E. Notts.	25	10	57	Leaving to join father at Cantonment – Aden.	
1100	30	4	57	Read Christine Margaret	Mrs J Read	West St. Childrey	None	29	3	52						
* 1101	21	1	57	Atkinson Terence	Mrs Atkinson	Chapel Way Childrey	None	22	5	52	None			?	Left district	
1102	20	4	57	Burls David George	Mrs R. Burls	Mount Pleasant Stow Hill Childrey	None	13	6	52	None					
1103	"	"	"	Adams Martin Bruce	Mrs Adams	Stow Hill, Childrey.	None	21	2	52	None			?	Left district.	
1104	"	"	"	Rowland Lawrence Kenneth George	Mrs K Rowland	Chapel Way Childrey	None	20	5	52	None					
1105	"	"	"	Holman Richard Charles	Mrs Holman	West Challow	None	28	2	51	None				Special School	
1107	13	5	57	Floyd Anthony Raymond	Mrs Ray John Floyd	Chapel Way, Childrey	None	4	7	52	None.					
1106.	7	5	57	Iles Norman.	c/o Mr B. Cilley	Chapel Way Childrey	None.	11	8	45	Harrow.	24	5	57	To Harrow. Returned Home.	
1108	20	5	57.	Pritchard Glyn	Mrs Margaret	c/o Mr & Mrs [illegible] East Challow	None	1	2	50	Elms Farm Infts. School Birmingham	7	6	57	Returned to Birmingham	Home address: [illegible] Birmingham.
1029	28	5	57	Smith Susan Mary	c/o Mr Brewer	The Crown Inn Childrey	None.	19	4	47	[illegible] Oldham	7	6	57	Returned home.	See also pages 11 & 12.
1109	25	3	57	Carter Christopher Francis	Mr Carter.	Chaude Mead West Challow	None.			50		23	7	57	Removing to Abingdon [illegible] Estate.	
1110	11	9	57	George Rita Mary	Mr George.	West Challow, Wantage	None	19	5	52.	None					
1111	"	"	"	Bailey Judith Rose	Mr Bailey	" " "	None.	2	6	52	None					
1112	"	"	"	Young Carole	Mr W. Young.	22 Chapel Way Childrey	None	21	11	52	None					
1113	"	"	"	Simmonds Peter Leslie	Mrs L. Simmonds	Chapel Way "	None.	6	10	52.	None.				Left District –	Grafton Lane C.P.
1114	"	"	"	Tucker William	Mrs W. Tucker	High St. Childrey	None.	19	10	52.	None.	20	10	57.	To R.A.F. Station Aden.	
1115	"	"	"	Vichman Janet Adelaide	Mr Vichman	Manor Flat Sparsholt	None	28	9	47.	None	} 23	7	58	To U.S.A.F Station	
1116.	"	"	"	Vichman Eugene	Mr Vichman	" " "	None.	19	10	49	None.				" " "	
1117	9	12	57.	Alaiston Janet	Mrs C J. Alaiston	2 Stow Hill Childrey	None.	9	12	49	Burghclere Newbury	23	7	58	Left district	
1118	7	1	58	Childerley Alison Lesley	Mr. K.F. Childerley	"Stone Cottage" Childrey	None	25	7	49	Burbage C.P. (Leics)	20	7 (12)	60 (57)	Icknield	
1119	"	"	"	Childerley Jonathan Scott	"		None	26	4	51	Burbage C.E. (Leics)	20	12	57.		
1120	"	"	"	Noviss Lesley Joan	Mr. L.A. Noviss	The Garage, Childrey	None	4	3	53	None				Convent, Abingdon	
1121	"	"	"	Wheeler Marlene Jane	Mr. H.J. Wheeler	Fettyplace Cottage	None	23	1	53	None					
1122	22	1	58	Stock Stephanie Janice	Mr J.R. Stock	The Crown Childrey	None	27	2	48	Bampton	4 / 20	12 / 12	59 / 57	Left district – Removing to Oxford	
1123	27	1	58	×Warriner Derek George	Mr. G.W. Warriner	Orchard Cottage	None	20	3	47	Prestatyn	21 / 21	7 / 7	58 / 58	22 7 58 Icknield	
1124	"	"	"	Warriner David Robert Paul		"	"	3	2	49	"	"		"	Removed to Kent	
1125	25	3	58	Barrett Patricia	Mr. A.H. Barrett	3 Stow Hill	None	3	8	47	Faringdon	21	3	58	} Removed to Lyford	
1126	"	"	"	Barrett Julie	"	"	None	11	11	51	"	"	"	"		
1127	23	4	58	England Cheryl Lyn ✓	Mr. G.W. England	Chapel Way Childrey	None	15	4	53	None					
1128				Rickens Linda Mary ✓	Mr. H.J. Rickens	~~High St~~ West St Childrey	None	26	4	53	"					
1129	"	"	"	Read Peter ✓	Mr. J.H. Read	West St Childrey	"	25	4	53						
1130	"	"	"	Johnson Alan Paul ✓	Mr. E.J.R. Johnson	3 Chapel Way Childrey	"	13	5	53						
1131	"	"	"	Smith Brian Gordon	Mr. G.C. Smith	2, West St Childrey	"	16	6	53						
1132	28	5	58	Freestone Paul Stanley Nicholas	Mr. F.H. Freestone	Corner Cottage	"	10	11	49	St. Mary's, Finstock	23 / 23	7 / 5	58 / 58	Returned to London	

* Number Entry slightly in error, according to Date

The Hatchet

Right to Left Lilian Pointer with bike William Froud (Bill) with white rabbit, -?- ?- Mr Froud, Violet Pointer -?-

The Cottage in the Hatchet Lane is very clear in this one

1 The Hatchet pub in Childrey about 1910 when the landlord was Basil Froud. The picture was taken by the well-known Victorian commercial photographer Frederick H.W. Ault.

The Hatchet 1903

Left to right
Trap Driver unknown, Nurse Girl with Lilian Pointer, Mr Ebenezer Pointer, ?, Mrs Nellie Pointer with William Pointer
The rest unknown. The tricycle at the side is a masterpiece and there is a small cottage up the Hatchet Lane

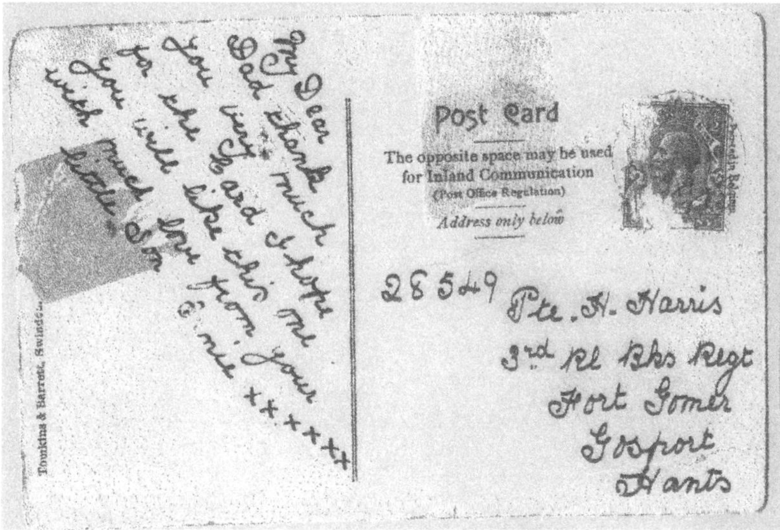

Writing to postcard below?

This picture is from a postcard sent by a boy to his father who lived in the house on the left. His mother is in the doorway and he is among the children in front of the pub.

Seven Men Killed Oxford and N. Berks Victims of Didcot Accident.

Seven men were killed and 13 other people seriously injured when a motor coach was involved in a collision with a railway truck which was being shunted at a level crossing at Didcot on Friday night. After finishing work, about 30 men and women were being taken home in the coach. They were in high spirits and some of them were singing, when suddenly there was a terrific crash. The bus was turned right over and the goods truck came to rest on top of it, pinning the passengers inside. The bus was completely wrecked and rescue work was most difficult. First-aid parties, doctors and ambulances from all round the area were summoned and the injured people, who were from Oxford and North Berks, were taken to the Radcliffe Infirmary. Among those who did good rescue and first-aid work were passengers in the bus who were lucky enough to escape with minor cuts and bruises or a shaking.

Basil Froud Hatchet Landlord

"Bus Tossed Over."

An eye-witness of the crash, who was walking nearby, told a reporter that it was just getting dusk when the incident happened.

"I could hear people singing in the back of the coach." he said, "and then came a terrific impact."

"The bus was literally tossed over on its side and the cries of the injured people were pitiful.

"Everyone in the vicinity hurried to the spot and did all they could to help, but there was not much which could be done for the injured, who were rushed to Oxford in a fleet of ambulances which quickly arrived on the scene."

Some of those who lost their lives were:-

Mr. Ernest Nobes, of 6, Council Houses, Upper Lambourn, bus-driver.
Mr. Ralph Whiteford, of 5, Council Houses, Upper Lambourn.
Mr Arthur Basil Froud, licensee of the Hatchet Inn, Childrey, Wantage.

Some of the most seriously injured passengers, all of whom were admitted to the Radcliffe Infirmary, are:-

Miss Alice Higginbotham, and her sister, Miss Elizabeth Higginbotham, of The Grotto, Childrey.
Other people injured included Mrs. Caroline Sims, of 23 West-Street, Childrey, and Mr. George Turner, of Corner Cottage, Childrey. Mrs. Sims received leg and head injuries but Mr. Turner escaped with minor injuries.

Childrey 1913

1939 Jockeys strike
Men probably kept their backs to the camera, because it was illegal to strike. The boys are Ron Rowland, Ivor Rowland, ? Cozens, Harry Cozens, Jackie Rowland, Dennis Rowland, Rodney Pike, Jackie Sheather.

1957

Mrs Froud at the Hatchet retirement party after 61yrs, with two of her oldest customers John Rowland and Soldier Rowland

Going Down Stowell

West view adjoining the Hatchet right both cottages demolished

At the bottom of Stowell Mount Pleasant hasn't changed a lot, but the cottages on the left are now tiled instead of thatched these days.
Look at the women and children round the pump on the left, no modcons in those days.
The cottages on the right were demolished in the 1930's

Charles Young Later in council house Chapel Way

Eli Young (Nigger) outside the cottage, now called Yeomans Cottage

Cress Cottage, now made into one. Mrs Pantin in the middle doorway 1928c.

CRESS COTTAGE, CHILDREY
Photo by Mrs. Price, Charlton W.I.

The same cottage on a snowy day. Back view from the cressbeds

Back to High Street

To walk past the Coffee Factory was a real treat and when it was sold in 1976 it was missed. It was hoped that the old peoples' bungalow would be built here, but it was not to be, and now Dolphin House is there - a lovely house.

The Coffee Factory 1968
At the back of the corner of West St.

Some people over stable door plus Miss Maynard and Miss French

Mrs. Bull, Mrs Cornish, Mrs Alder, Phillis Legge

Walking on down the village

The shop when it was Treadwells 1915. Who are the men and boys?

Can you imagine meat carcasses hanging today

1926 Post Office at Penn House The Legge family, right -left Ben, Ruth, Janet, baby Mary

Old barn at top of Stowell, near Tudor House.

Coming up out of the other Stowell access Charles Cottage 1910.
Before Coventry Almshouses were built.

March 1934 approx

4 Generations of Soldier Rowlands family taken at Coventry Almshouses
Back, Granny (Goosey) Hutt, daughter Annie Rowland (nee Hutt)
Mrs. Beckett (tenant) holding Sheila Rowland Great grandaughter

1915 Look at the pump in front. Is this a postman or milkman? there are several options.

CHILDREY. THE ALMSHOUSES

Walk on down Village

The Old Thatch. Before 1912 as the farm wall is still on the right hand side where the Coventry Almshouse were built in 1912

Before the phone box. The little girl is Phillis Barton 1928c

Ealand Alder in the garden of Symonds Farm c1915

Lesters Cottage September 1959 and Winter 1981-2

I sneaked this one in because of the snow

Pond Farm c1910

c1915. Winter
A real swan! No phone box

Before the Reading Room and First World War. (No War Memorial) The original is dated 1880. There are massive trees by the pond and no rails on the road side.

c1910 Electricity has arrived but the post is a bit crooked

Before the Reading Room. Look at the Ricks to the side of Hazeldene. No Chapel Way then 1889. I wonder if rails were put on top of low wall in the front to stop boys sitting on it. (Photo courtesy OCC Photography Archive)

The building of the Reading Room. The chapel still has wooden gates at side at this time.
(Photos courtesy OCC Photography Archive)

The village now has a Reading Room and Lesters is being thatched. Perhaps it gave every one a boost as they came of of recession. Also, new white posts on the pond. (Photo courtesy OCC Photography Archive)

1910 - 1915

Tree dead by pond. No War Memorial but after Reading Room.

Front and back of Rose-Lea no 1 and 2 as its known now.

Back view from Frouds Farmyard.
(Photos courtesy OCC Photography Archive)

1918 at least.

Can anyone remember the phone box being white?

The lovely old Methodist Chapel 1914, with wooden gates before the iron ones were fixed and its later collapse. But of course now there is the splendid new one.

Chapel Cottage 1888 approx.

At Chapel Cottages 1927-8
L-R Mr Bungay, Mrs Bungay, Mick Lewis, Mrs Lucy Lewis, L Barton
Front Reg Bungay and sister, and Louis Lane
Reg Bungay in front died a hero. Mrs Lewis lived at No 1 and Bungays at No 2.

1916 approx.
Mrs V Booker (Organist) Olive, Marjorie and Norah
Chapel Cottage.

The Heros

Fuel is drained from Lambourn wrecked tanker.

Work began early today on emptying the tanker, carrying 2,500 gallons of jet fuel, which crashed into two shops and overturned in Lambourn yesterday.
The centre of the town was sealed off by the police from the main crossroads to the junction of Oxford Street and Broadway. Another tanker drained about 1,200 to 1,500 gallons of the remaining fuel from the vehicle.
While the draining off was done, firemen stood by with foam equipment and water pumps in case of fresh outbreaks of fire.
Last night, firemen with two appliances - the Lambourn major pump and the special foam tender from Reading stood by. The firemen spent the night clearing away debris from the two most badly damaged cottages, carrying out the work by the light of large paraffin spot lamps.

CABLE MELTED

During the night Post Office workmen worked on the lines to restore subscribers' telephones.
Nineteen subscribers' wires and one fire wire were put out of action.
After the accident the heat melted the main cable and it ran into a pool at the foot of the telephone pole opposite the Broadway.
Hungerford Rural Council declared unsafe the shop of Mr. Edwards, a second hand trader and this morning workmen dislodged tiles and masonry at the top of the building in order to lessen the weight.
The floors were leaning down into the street and there were great cracks in the walls.
Fourteen families were made homeless.
The driver of the tanker, Mr. Reginald Bungay (36) of Jennings Street, Swindon, died before he could be taken from the lorry's cab. He had remained at the wheel as the vehicle ran out of control down Hungerford Hill.

WATER IS SAFE

The drinking water supply in the area has not been contaminated. Mr. Eric Rippin, manager of Lambourn Valley Water Works confirmed today.
"Slight discolouration noticeable in the water is due to extra pressure in the mains caused by use of fire-hoses" he said.
From one of the damaged houses, the residents took wedding presents which had been given to Miss Sadie Harries who was married last Saturday. She is on honeymoon.
For Avril Read (12) it was the second narrow escape within a year. While in the bedroom yesterday with her mother, Mrs. Joan Read, the building shook and the front wall fell out ino the road leaving the floor at a precarious angle.
While at Farnborough air show last year, she was nearby when an aircraft crashed, killing a number of people, including three close to her.
Those who visited the scene of the accident today included the Lord Lieutenant of Berkshire (Mr. H A Benyon) the Chief Constable of Berkshire (Cmdr. the Hon Humphry Legge), and Supt. W.S Brooks (officer in charge of the Newbury Police Division).

60 m.p.h. TERROR-ON-WHEELS STRIKES A QUIET VILLAGE

OIL-BLAZE DRIVER DIES SAVING OTHERS

By ARTHUR COOK

The main street was set alight. Shop fronts were ripped open. Eight cottages went up in flames. Even the river became an inferno. *But only one man died.*

And last night, in explosion-wrecked Lambourn, Berks, every villager spoke in praise of that one man -"the man who lost his life trying to save us" they said.

His name was Reginald Bungay. He was 36. He lived in Jennings Street, Swindon. He was a bridegroom of only a fortnight. He was also the driver of a 2,500-gallon jet fuel tanker.

It was 12.35pm., lunch time in the sleepy racing village of Lambourn when Reginald Bungay lost control of his eight wheel tanker. He was then travelling down the mile-long Hungerford Hill that leads to the village centre. The out-of-control tanker gathered speed. Driver Bungay could have jumped - but he didn't.

Soon he was careering towards the village at 60 miles an hour. He set his horn blaring to warn villagers. He shouted, too, as he tried to weave his paraffin laden tanker to safety. He knew what would happen if he crashed. He knew what would happen to the village. But the speed was too much for driver Bungay.

As he roared through the village and tried to take a corner his 20-ton tanker crashed into a line of shops, ripped the fronts bare and cannoned off down the road.

There it smashed into four cottages, overturned and exploded its 2,500 gallons of fuel over the village. Driver Bungay died at the wheel.

In a few seconds Lambourn was transformed into a wartime blitz scene. A fountain of blazing fuel spilled down the main street, setting fire to cottages and the near-by river

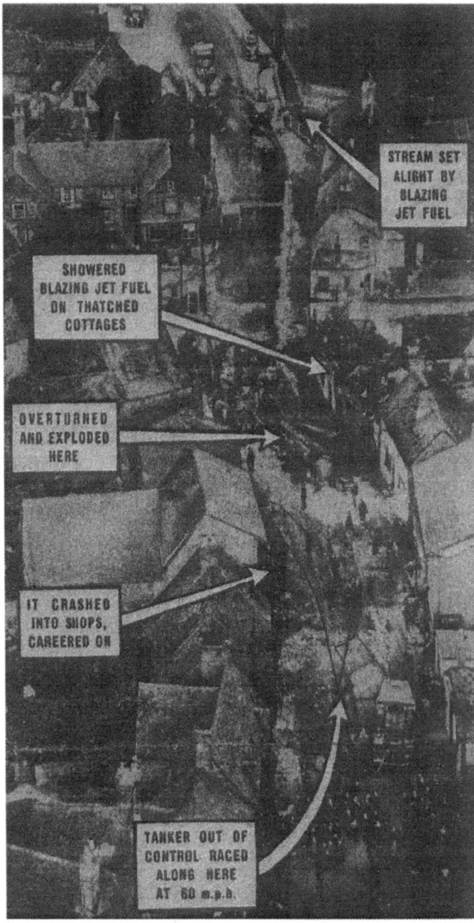

How Havoc came to Lambourn yesterday
A Daily Express picture from the air.

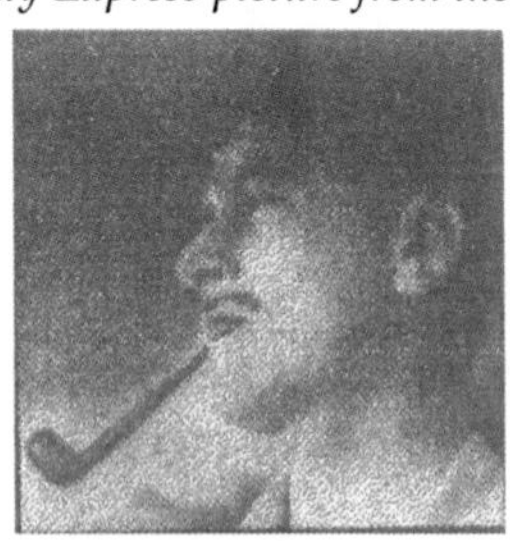

DRIVER REGINALD BUNGAY
Married only a fortnight.

Herbert Samual Vaughan (Mick)
of Chapel Cottage

A Prisoner of War
Gunner Herbert Lewis, of Childrey

Gunner Herbert Samuel Vaughan (Mick) Lewis, the only son of Mrs Lewis, of Chapel Cottages, Childrey, near Wantage, and of the late Mr. S. G. Lewis, who, ten weeks ago was reported missing is now stated to be a prisoner at Camp Stalag, Germany.
Aged 32, Gunner Lewis was called up as a Reservist on the outbreak of war, and soon afterwards went to France. Married with a son and a daughter, his wife lives at Maidstone. For some time he worked at Challow Engineering Works, and has recently been working at a paper mills in Kent.
In earlier life he was well known in the Wantage district as a footballer.

Turn towards Church

Bartons at Orchard House
Back Row: John Barton, Mr Barton (Snr), Mick Lewis, Bill Barton, Ted Barton, Bert Barton
Front Row: Beatrix Barton, ?, Mrs Barton.

Orchard House 1933
Mrs & Mrs Barton and their oldest daughter Beatrix

Next to Orchard House, seen in the background, Mary Simmonds ne Bull moved here as a child, when her father came as a much needed tractor driver.

1928 In the background Fettiplace Almshouses and the teachers house. The ivy covered cottages were pulled down for stone cottage to be built that is now called Rosemarys Cottage. When I was a child, the biggest adder I have ever seen came out from under the pond on the left. I was with three other children. We were terrified.

A lovely shady corner before we go up to the church.

Entrance to Cantoris House. There was a terrible fuss because the barn was stripped and a tin roof put on.

Starting up Church Street
These cottages opposite Cantoris House were pulled down 1935 - 38.

A Childrey Wedding September 16th 1933

Mr. H. V.S. Lewis and Miss Beatrice Barton

There were five bridesmaids at the wedding of Miss Beatrice Ethel Mary Barton to Mr. Herbert Vaughan Samuel Lewis, which took place on Saturday at St. Mary's Church, Childrey. The bride is the daughter of Mr. and Mrs. J Barton, of Orchard House, Childrey, and the grand-daughter of the late Mr. Henry Cox, of Childrey, and the bridegroom is the son of Mrs. Lewis and the late Sergeant Lewis, of Chapel Cottages, Childrey.

The bride wore a dress of ivory satin and a coronet of orange blossom, a tulle veil (lent by an aunt and worn by the bride's mother and two aunts at their weddings), a pearl necklace with diamond clasp, and white satin shoes. Her bouquet was composed of pink carnations and fern.

The chief bridesmaid was Miss Phyllis Barton (sister of the bride), and the other attendants were the Misses Alma Cox, Gertie Farmer and the Misses Rene Humphries and Eileen Brown. They all wore pale green dresses of organdie, white picture hats, lace mittens and white satin shoes. They had pink crystal necklaces and carried bouquets of pink pentstemons.

Mr J. Barton (late of Metropolitan Police) gave his daughter away. The officiating clergyman was the Rev. Herbert Sheppard (rector of Childrey), and the best man was Mr. B. Lewis, of Calne (brother of the bridegroom).

The service was fully choral and the hymns, chosen by the bride were "Lead us, Heavenly Father, lead us'" and "Love Divine, all loves excelling."

A reception was held at Orchard house, and amongst the guests received by Mr. and Mrs. Barton were Mrs. Lewis (the bridegroom's mother), Messrs. John, William, Edward, Albert,

Cont. on page 124

On now to the Church

c. 1915 The font decorated for Harvest Festival

1915 Inside the church before the first world war was over (no war memorials). Don't the lamps look lovely they were filled with oil.

A front and back view.
The trees are very small at the back.
Year Unknown.

For over 50 years or until death doth them part what a marvelous achievement

Circa 1918 These are Childrey people but not our church.
Back Row: Mrs And, Mr Bert Broad, Mr Simpson ? ? ? Charlie Fleetwood
Front Row: Mrs Simpson, Mrs Broad, Ernest Richards (Groom), Eva Broad (Bride), Fanny Broad, later Fleetwood, Mr Broad Snr.
Children sitting: Dennis Broad, Donald Broad.

Gwendoline Lewis of Chapel Cottage Childrey to Mr Leonard Shaw of Grove. In the playground of the Methodist Sunday School after.
March 1935

Mr. H.V.S. Lewis and Miss Beatrice Barton
September 16th, 1933

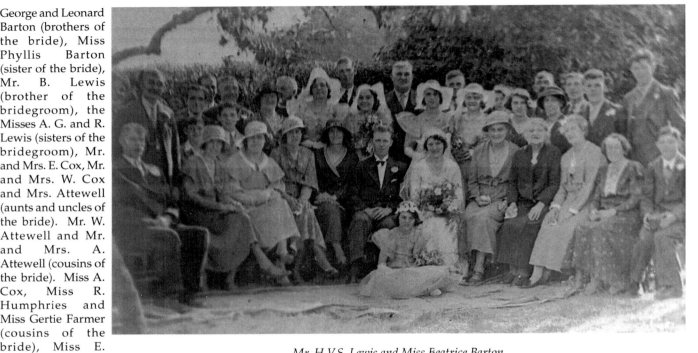

George and Leonard Barton (brothers of the bride), Miss Phyllis Barton (sister of the bride), Mr. B. Lewis (brother of the bridegroom), the Misses A. G. and R. Lewis (sisters of the bridegroom), Mr. and Mrs. E. Cox, Mr. and Mrs. W. Cox and Mrs. Attewell (aunts and uncles of the bride). Mr. W. Attewell and Mr. and Mrs. A. Attewell (cousins of the bride). Miss A. Cox, Miss R. Humphries and Miss Gertie Farmer (cousins of the bride), Miss E. Brown (friend of the bride), Mr. and Mrs. J Booker and Mr. and Mrs. V. Booker (uncles and aunts of the bridegroom), Mr V. Booker and the Misses Nina, Nora, Joyce, June, Nellie and Peggy Booker (cousins of the bridegroom). Mr. and Mrs Mahoney (friends of the bride). Mrs Gane (cousin of the bridegroom), and Mr L. Smith (friend of the bride).

EASTER - LEWIS

The wedding took place at St. Mary's Church, Childrey on Saturday, of Miss Irene Olive Lewis, the youngest daughter of the late Sergt. G. Lewis and of Mrs. L. Lewis, of Childrey, and Mr. Albert Charles Easter and the late Mrs. Easter, of Salisbury.
The Rector (the Rev. W.F.J.G. Coles) officiated and Miss Ethel Heading was at the organ for the hymns, "The Voice that breathed o'er Eden" and "Love Divine, all Loves Excelling." Given away by her brother (Mr. V. Lewis), the bride wore a satin beaute dress, with veil and wreath of orange blossom, white satin shoes and stockings to match. She carried a bouquet of carnations.
The bridesmaids were Miss Gwendoline Lewis (sister of the bride), the Misses Alice and Dolly Easter (sisters of the bridegroom), and Miss Sybil Shaw, of Grove. They wore mauve crepe-de-chine dresses, with head-dresses and pink shoes and carried bouquets of pink tulips. They were given bracelets of the occasion.
Mr. V. Easter (brother of the bridegroom) was best man.
After a reception in the Parish Room Mr. and Mrs. Easter left for their honeymoon at Folkestone. The bride travelled in a brown coat, rust-coloured dress and brown accessories. They are to live at Maidstone.

Nelly Wheeler to Potter Collins
older bridesmaids, Joyce Edmonds and Ruby Stone
3 small ones, Mary Bull, Dorothy Collins, Janet Giles.
Harry Bennett. Best Man c.1939

Wedding of Miss Cox

The marriage took place on Saturday afternoon at the Church of St. James the Less, East Hanney, of Mr. Philip Edgar Froud, youngest son of Mrs Froud and the late Mr. Edward Froud, of Pond Farm, Childrey, and Miss Lena May Cox, youngest daughter of Mr. and Mrs. G. Cox of 1 Steventon Road, East Hanney. The bride wore a dress of white taffeta and veil and a coronet of orange blossom and carried a bouquet of dark red carnations. The bridesmaid was her friend, Miss Hilda Prior, and the Rev. F L. Wheeler officiated.

X

1944 Bert Rowland to Flossie Comely.

Mr. & Mrs. J. Rowland, *Mr. & Mrs. Comley*

1944 Wedding of Bob Cowie to Nellie Mason of Greendown.
Best man, Ted Cowie, bridesmaid bride's sister Winnie Mason.
The bride was given away by her brother Ernest Mason.
The Mason girls used to walk from Green Down to Childrey School every day

July 1948 West Challow
Wedding of Miss Clanfield to Mr. James Anthony Devlin.
The bride was attended by Miss D. Clanfield and Mr. R George as best man.

April 1949 Mr. Percy Kenneth Leslie Rowland to Miss. Sylvia May Pullman

Oct 1948 Miss. June M. Mullineux to Mr. William Young of Childrey, at the Emmaual Church in the Wirrold

Nov 1948 Mr. Ronald George Rowland, a well known member of the Childrey United Football Club was married on Saturday at St Mary's Church to Miss Dorothy Myra Rowland. The bride was attended by Miss June Rowland, Miss Sheila Rowland and Miss Maureen Wilken

1948 The wedding took place on Saturday at the Methodist Church Childrey of Mr.Reginald Colin Jefferies to Miss Sylvia Elsie Turner

Dec 1949
L-R Mrs. Simmonds, Pauline Whitworth, Mick Simmons, Sylvia Dowers, Leslie Simmons bridegroom, Mary Bull bride, Ben Bull father, Janet Giles, Mrs. Bull mother
Front Margaret Bull brides sister

August 1951
Miss Pamela Joan Rowland to
Sub-Lieut Alan John Stafford, R.N.

April 1950 Swinford Man's Childrey Bride
Mr. Raymond John Floyd to Miss Doreen L. Alder. Wearing a white crepe gown with a veil and headdress of orange blossom, the bride carried a bouquet of red carnations, lilies of the valley and trailing fern. She was attended by the Misses Pat andIris Alder and Gladys Evans

Bert Dance | *Sheila Rowland* | *Oct 1953 The Wedding of Mr.Louis Cohen to Peggy Rowland* | *Joan Rowland* | *Mrs & Mr J Rowland*

Jan 1954 Horseshoe for Childrey bride
Miss Barbara Isobel Hannaby to Mr. Ivor Vivian Rowland

18 Sept 1954 Miss Shelia Rowland and Mr. Frances Gorden Cox
The Rector, the Rev. W.F.J.G. Coles offciated and the wedding was the last one he will conduct as Rector of Childrey as he is leaving to become Vicar of Mapledurham.

1955 Miss Elsie Simpson to Mr Bert Rowland

1955 Lucky Golden Sovereign in Wantage bride's shoe.
When Miss. Christine Elizabeth Alder walked into the Parish Church of St. Peter and St Paul at Wantage for her wedding on Saturday. She had a golden sovereign in her right shoe - placed there for luck by her father. Miss Alder was married to Mr.Graham John McGregor the Childrey United Football Club goalkeeper

Mervyn Rowland and his wife Maureen.
Married at Uffington

July 1956 Miss Lorna Vandervell to Mr. G. Hall

Guests Mrs. Florence Booker grandmother.
Lucy Hardman Aunt.

Mr. Jack Booker with his daughter in law and grandchildren

More Guests at Hall - Vandervell wedding Penny Wixey, nee Booker with her daughter and Ruby Johns nee Booker

28th March 1959 Miss Stella Vandervell and Mr. Thomas Whittle

April 1956 Dorothy Collins to Harold Huitt
At the back Percy Collins, Best man Ron Rowland Mrs. P. Collins
Front L-R Bridesmaids 1. 2. Marlyn Simmons, 3. Marion Young, 4. Sandra Breakspeare,
5. Carol Young, 6. Wendy Cully, 7. Denise Rowland.

Miss Olive Booker to Mr Tom Cox
the Misses Booker were bridesmaids
Year not known

Wedding of ??
L-R Rosie Froud, Lesley Lay, Charles Lay, Ellen Froud, Olive ?

April 1973 The wedding took place at the United Reformed Church, Headington Oxford of Mr. Douglas Legge Of West Street Childrey and Miss Carol Clements of Headington

Devizes I can't find a date for this wedding, but it's of an old school friend Miss Janet Giles to Mr. Hedley Craig, Mr Giles and Bridesmaid Joyce Giles (Cousin)

Entertainment

June 16 1960 Laughing Flower Girl at Childrey Church Fete

Christine Rowland (left) finds a ready sale for her buttonholes at Childrey Church fete in the grounds of Childrey Rectory on Saturday. With her are (left to right) Jacqueline Brewer, Veronica Smith and Elizabeth O'Higgins.

They say it's a safe job
So that the photographer could get a real look at his disguise Ronald Rowland, of West Street, Childrey, temporarily forsook the safety of the wire netting at Childrey Church fete's Aunt Sally on Saturday. Mr C. Brown looks on as a visitor prepares to throw.

Strong Arm and Keen Eye
Driving a nail into a block of oak caused a lot of fun at the Church fete held at Childrey Rectory on Saturday. - E.A. 1956 Stella Vandervell after her marriage to Tom Whittle enjoying themselves at the fete Left to right Ken Rowland, Ron Rowland, ? ? George Wylie, Danny & Mrs Vandervelle, Tom Whittle groom and his wife Stella, poss young John Whelpdale

c. 1935
1 Driver Mr Chandler, 2 Florrie Burls, 3 Mrs Buckley
1 Mrs Kitty Pointer, 2 Mrs Ellis, 3 Mrs Gibbs 4 Mrs Florrie Booker, 5 Mrs Annie Rowland, 6 Joyce Gardener, 7 Mrs Williams, 8 Ruth Legge, 9 Mrs Males, 10 Mrs Mackey Rae, 11 Janet Legge, 12 Ivy Froud,
1, June Ellis, 2 John Sheather, 3 Beryl Pointer, 4 Sheila Rowland, 5 Barbara Gibbs, 6 Mabel Sheather, 7 Nellie Mason, 8 ? Embling, 9 Mrs Embling, 10 Mrs Panting.

A Christmas party in the Reading Room
Run by L - R standing 1 Mrs Mary Bennett, 2 Harry Males, 3 Mr Winterbourne, 4 Mr Harry Bennett, 5 ?, 6 Rev Coles, 7 Mr Trinder
Sitting L - R ?, Mrs Kitty Ellis

Dancing Class presents - The Teddy Bears Picnic
Front Bernie Belf - Marilyn Simmonds ? Miss Christine Rowland Marian Young
Felicity Simpson

Dancing Class presents "The Teddy Bears Picnic"
Back Row ? ? ? Margaret Bull ? ? ?
Front Bernie Belf - ? Moss - Marion Young, Marilyn Simmons - Christine Rowland

Red Riding Hood
Mrs Bull Ruth Pottinger Belle Aldridge

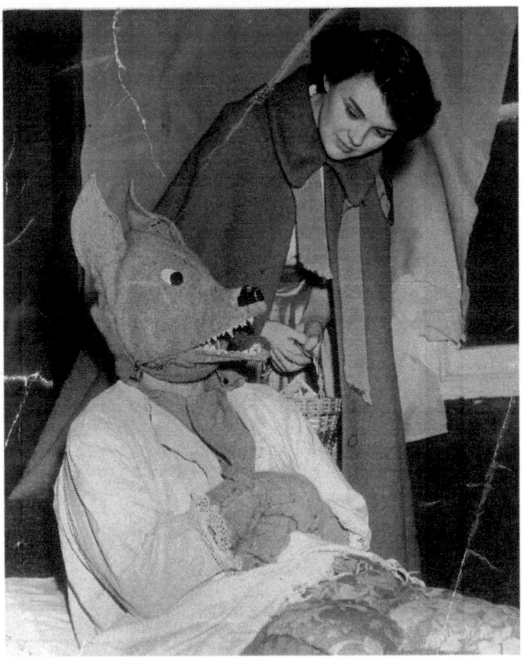

Ruth Pottinger as Red Riding Hood

Cinderella
R - L Mrs Bull, Mrs Bennett, Pat Hannaby, June Young, Mrs Ellis, Arthur Reed

Babes in the Wood
Peter Ellis, Belle Aldridge, Joy & Ruth Pottinger, Margaret Bull

Sport

Childrey Football Club 1907 - 8
Back Row L - R 1 Jack Booker, 2 ?, 3 ?, 4 ?, 5 Sheather, 6, Billie Hitchcock
Centre Row 1 ?, 2 ?, 3 ?, Bert Broad, 5, ?
Front Row 1 ?, 2 ?

1920 - 21 Football
Back Row 1 Bill Hunt, 2 Happy Harris, 3 ?, 4 Mr Dunn, 5 Reg Rowland,
6 Vicar Mr McCramm, 7 Mr Mills, 8 D Hack
Centre Row 1 Frank Young, 2 Mr Pettifer, 3 ?, 4 ?, 5 Bert Ballard, 6 Midge Kench, 7 ? Haines
Front 1 ? Young, 2 Les Dance

Childrey School Juniors

Goalie approx 1921
Back Row L - R B?. Mr Mills?, ?, Edward Froud, ?
Middle Row, Dennis Broad, ?, ? Dowse, Les Embling, ?,
Front Row ?, Robert Heading, ?

1930 - 31
L - R Back Row 1 Midge Kench, 2 Bert Lewis, 3 Bob Heading, 4 Bill Hicks, 5 ?, 6 Potter Collins, 7 ?, 8 ?, 9 Bimmy Rea, 10 Harry Bennett
Middle Row 1 Percy Collins, 2 Bert Booker, 3 ?, 4 Bert Dance, 5 Les Embling, 6 Vaughan Booker, 7 Mr Shepherd Vicar
Sitting 1 ?, 2 ?, 3 G Needham

Saturday, April 12, 1924.

Mr. A. B. Woodley presided at the tea to which the players and officials were subsequently entertained at "The Crown and Thistle," being supported by messrs. E. T. Lessings, M.P., W. Bernthal, J. A. Greenwood, T. W. Pratley and W. Tilley (Newbury).

The CHAIRMAN, congratulating the Childrey team upon its success, said the game had been a real cup-tie, fought out strenuously right up to the last, neither side giving any quarter nor expecting it, being out to win for their side. It was a pleasure to be able to congratulate Childrey on winning the cup, because the previous year, they had got into the final, and on that occasion they put up an excellent show against a much stronger team than themselves. Whilst they all agreed that Childrey had proved themselves the better team that afternoon, he was sure they would join with him in sympathising with Didcot, who had had to fight practically the whole of the game, with the exception of five or ten minutes, with ten men, which had severely handicapped them, since the player Didcot had lost held the key position in the team, i.e., centre-half, and to lose a man in any game sometimes meant all the difference between winning and losing. They were very sorry indeed, for the Didcot team, and for the player who had been injured, but he hoped they would take heart, and, perhaps next year, they would come up again and lift the trophy. One thing he felt he should explain, was that it was the first year they had been unable to give medals to the runners-up. As they knew competitions at the present time cost a lot of money, and during the last two years thay had been faced with a deficit, and had not been able to accumulate sufficient funds to give two sets of medals. At the annual meeting it had been decided that they must retrench, and it had been submitted to the clubs, who had agreed that for this year, at any rate, the runners-up medals should be foregone: but Didcot, having won the cup once, would not be so disappointed as a team who had never been in the final previously. Childrey had lifted the cup for the first time, and Didcot were good enough sportsmen to congratulate them. Mr. Woodley then welcomed Mr. E. A. Lessing, whose uncle was the donor of the cup. Mr. Woodley expressed the hope that Mr. Lessing would convey to Mr. Strauss the appreciation of clubs in North Berks of the trophy he had given them. It had been competed for since 1907, since when it had been the ambition of every club to have its name inscribed on the shield at least once. The past season had seen thirty-seven entries, which equalised the previous best number, whilst there were two thousand players registered as ready to turn out to do battle for the cup on behalf of their club and village, so that from that Mr. Strauss would be able to realise the amount of pleasure and sport his splendid gift had provided.

Cup Final 1924 Didcot v. Childrey

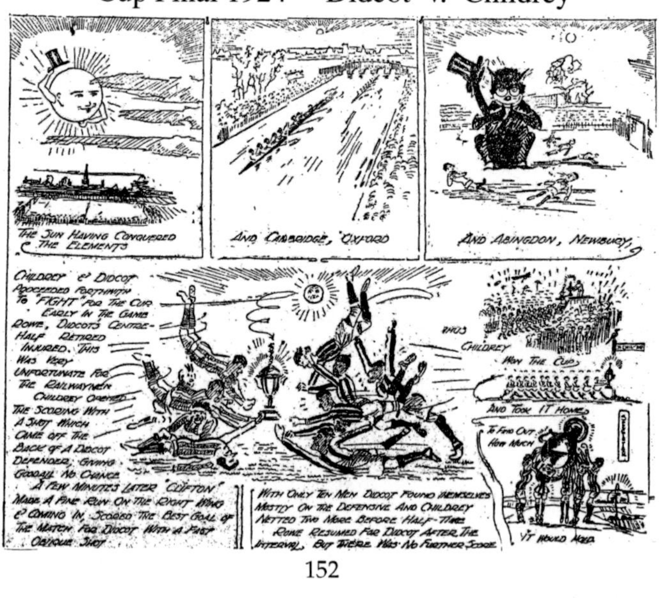

1923 - 4

?, ? Dowse, Vaughan Booker

1 ?, 2 ?, 3 ?, 4 Jimmy Hammond, 5 Bim Rae, 6 Mr Shepherd Vicar, 7 Ray Bishop, 8 ?, 9 Dance, 10 Mr Embling, 11 ? Froud, 12 ?, 13 Edgar Pottinger

1 ?, 2 Charlie Lester, 3 ? Coward, 4 Bill Rowland, 5 Bert Broad, 6 Sid Rowland, 7 Les Embling?, 8 Mr Dunn, 9 Jack Booker

1, Les Booker, 2 ? Booker, 3 Taffy Ayres, 4 B Hicks, 5 ?

C 1943
Back Row (Trainer) H Bennett, A Read, F Breakespear, C. Greenaway, R Rowland, C Cornish, J Rowland E Pottinger
Front Row P. Collins, B Booker, H Males, D Greenaway, K Rowland, A Rowland, (Midge) Kench

1948-9
Back Row 1 Pete Dance, 2 P Wyatt, 3 Bert Rowland, 4 Bas Hunt, 5 Dave Symonds, 6 D Pendle, 7 Stan Simpson, 8 Mick Simmonds
Front Row 1 John Kent, 2 Mervyn Rowland, 3 John Sheather, 4 Dennis Wise, 5 Tom Carter

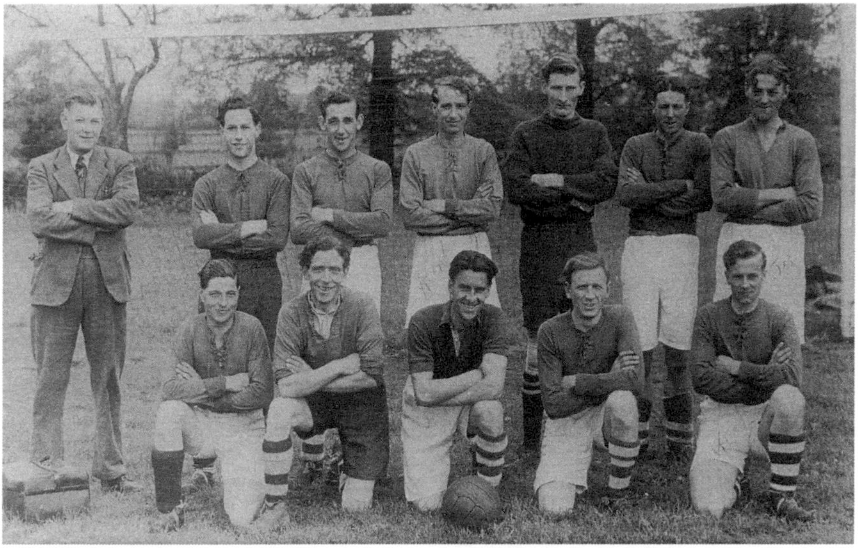

Back Row Harry Bennetts, Alan Reed, Fred Breakspeare, Ron Rowland
B Moran - Bert & Joe Rowland
Front Row ? poss John Westmacott, 2 Bert Booker, 3 Dixie Greenaway, 4 Harry Males,
5 Ken Rowland

Back Row Aubrey Keep, Harry Bennett, Alan Read, Ron Rowland, Ivor Rowland,
Jack Timmins, Bert Rowland
Front Row John Kent, Ron Matthews, Den Rowland, Bert Rowland, Ken Rowland

C 1959 G Carter, M Rowland, R Hannaby, P Lester, S.T. Alder, T McGregor
Chris Cornish, R Matthews, R Rowland, P Hannaby, D Green
Players in the Faringdon Thursday Memorial Cup

L - R Fred Breakspeare, Colin Greenaway, Bill Young

1 Harry Bennet, 2 Alan Lines, 3 Herbie Richens, 4 Ron Rowland, 5 ?, 6 Rodney Pike, 7 Alf Watts
1 Joe Green, 2 Ted johnson, 3 ? Tony McGregor, 4 Charlie Brown, 5 David Green

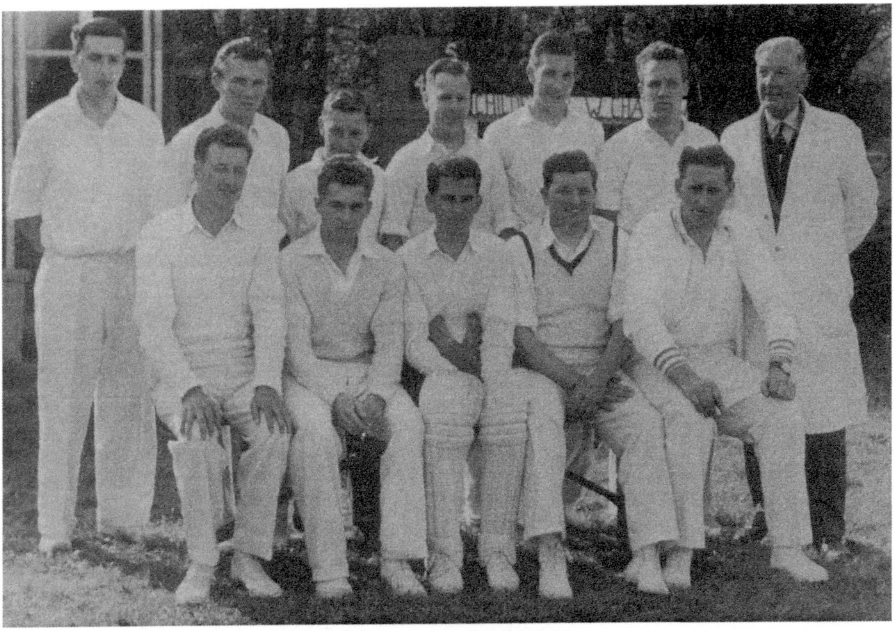

Childrey & West Challow
L - R Back Row 1 Claude Bosley, 2 Spicer ?, 3 Robin Haines, 4 Sid Alder, 5 Tony McGregor, 6 Aubrey Haines, 7 Henry Bennett
Front Row 1 Jack Bosley, 2 Don Bert, 3 Danny Vandervell, 4 Bert Rowland, 5 Rodney Pike

Mystery

Tug of War
This is the only tug-of-war picture and only one man identified
Herbert Vaughan Lewis (Mick)

Groups

Babies Ron and Bert. Twins with their mother Annie Rowland and her parents-in-law
Mr & Mrs W Rowland.
Manor Cottages West St 1922

Birthday
Mrs Bull, Mrs Giles, Janet Middleton (sitting), Mrs Williams

The Wood Yard - next to Pond House
Mrs Comley, Flossie (nee Comley) and husband Bert Rowland, Mr Comley and children Pauline and Anthony

Workers from La. Novis' Garage
Back row, L - R Standing Richard Elbrow
Middle Row, Steve Devlin, Marion Young, Peter Males, June Young, Standing Sue Wheeler & Derek Mills
Front Row, Leslie Rowland, Peter Brown, Mike Brown, Stuart Males.

1 ?, 2 ?, 3 Mrs Gauld, 4 Mrs Frank Young, 5 ?, 6 Frank Young, 7 Mrs Richens, 8 Nelly Young Child Herbie Richens

Left to Right Mrs Williams, May Bennett, Mrs Richens, Mrs Harris

Aggie Froud, later Mrs Somerville

Left to Right
Mrs Hack (nee Legge) school teacher
Mrs Bellinger, Mr Bellinger
(of Bellingers Garage, Mill Street)
Mrs Lucy Lewis, nee Booker
at a fancy dress dance as gypsies and Rajah

Mr Bert Booker at the workshop
next to Lesters

Mrs Emma Ballard and Mrs Lucy Lewis
outside Hazeldene 1930

CHAPEL OUTING
It's nearly sixty years since Mrs Corkery went on this outing from Wantage. She's on the left in the black trunks!

Mr & Mrs Broad
the other girl in front is Sylvia Turner

Thomas and Emma Collins
Chapel Way Council Houses

Young Family about 1900 - 1910
Left to right, back row, Charles, Margery, Frank, Amos, Eli or Nigger Mary Annie
Front Row, George, Mary nee Pettifer

Workers at the Foundry Nalder & Nalder
B Kent, Albert Kent, Charlie Lester, Bert Giles, Frank Alder, Syd Row, Bill Brooker
Tommy Fleetwood, Bink? Winterbourne, Eddy Fleet, Jack Moss, Ted Johnson
1934
Information given by Jack Moss now aged 84

A Day Out
L - R Eva Fulbrook, Mrs Breakspeare, Ann Winterbourne, Mr Bert Winterbourne,
Mr Ben Bull, Mrs Mary Bull

Mercy Ebsworth
born 1863 Childrey 1st wife of Samuel G Lewis
Her father was a coal porter at Childrey in 1871

Mr St Pere, ?, Grampy Young, Betty St Pere

Ellen Rea nee Ballard died 1916 aged 76
Bertha Froud nee Rea died 1917 aged 90

Mystery
possibly Mrs Marchant

Mr & Mrs Jack Gibbs a well known couple in Childrey for many years

The Flying Scotsman passing through Challow Station at the bottom of the New Road or Station Road as its called.

Agriculture

and all the work the horses done, as well as men

Eli (Nigger) Young Ploughman 1930
Look how his legs fly up round the corners, although small, he was an excellent ploughman.
(Photo courtesy of The University of Reading)

Seeding the old way
Ernie Mason & John Newman c1930 East Challow in the background
(Photo courtesy of The University of Reading)

Curly Frouds cows, a cozy home
(Photo courtesy of The University of Reading)

A bit of a traffic jam in c1950

Possibly Mr Froud or Mr Tomlin, who was the carter for Pond Farm
(Photo courtesy of The University of Reading)

All the jobs the horses done
Nell & Potter Collins

Grampy Froud (Edward) called Dick

Mr Pantin
Flossie Comley (Sen)

SPARSHOLT 1
B4001 CHALLOW STN 2
FARINGDON 8
LETCOMBE BASSETT 2 B4001
LAMBOURN 6½
CHILDREY CHURCH
NO THROUGH ROAD

The Way Out

Childrey Rampagnes Manor 1915

Women's Institute c. 1948 at the Manor
Back Row Barbara Hannaby, Mrs Hannaby, ?, Mrs Flo Booker, R Simpson, ?, ?, Janet Middleton
Middle Row ?, Joy Pottinger, Ivy Froud, ?, Belle Aldridge, P Bedford, ?, ?, ?, ?, ?
Front Row Mrs Simpson, Mrs Giles, ?, Mrs Leigh, Mrs Bull, Mrs Skinner, Eileen Smith,
Mrs Soldier Rowland, Ruth Pottinger

The Rectory 1915
A lovely view much lighter than most people remember, but of course the trees were smaller